810

M-836

A NEW ENGLAND GROUP AND OTHERS

SHELBURNE ESSAYS
ELEVENTH SERIES

A New England Group And Others

SHELBURNE ESSAYS
ELEVENTH SERIES

By Paul Elmer More

BOSTON AND NEW YORK
Houghton Mifflin Company
The Riverside Press Cambridge

Advertisement

OF the essays in this volume which have already appeared in print *Emerson* and *Jonathan Edwards* were published originally in *The Cambridge History of American Literature; Charles Eliot Norton* in the *Nation; Evolution and the Other World* in the *Harvard Theological Review; Henry Adams, Samuel Butler of Erewhon, Viscount Morley, Economic Ideals,* and *Oxford, Women, and God* in the *Unpopular* (now the *Unpartizan*) *Review.* Some of these essays have been considerably altered and enlarged for the present publication. *The Spirit and Poetry of Early New England* was delivered at the Johns Hopkins University as one of the Turnbull lectures.

Contents

THE SPIRIT AND POETRY OF
EARLY NEW ENGLAND

A New England Group
and Others

• •

THE SPIRIT AND POETRY OF EARLY
NEW ENGLAND

THE refuge of the Puritans on this side of the ocean was not exactly a nest of singing birds; but it had a character and self-conscious spirit which sought expression in verse as well as in sermons, and, at least, if not poetical, it resounded with the psalmody of the saints. In judging the strength and weakness of those early poets, to grant them the title by courtesy, we should remember first of all that for the most part they belonged to the class who were leaders in breaking away from the full current of English life, and spoke for a people who brought with them to these lands a civilization rent and shorn by what rightly may be called one of the huge mischances of history.

It is, I know, the teaching of a certain school of scientific historians that the changes of civilization are produced by large impersonal laws under whose sway the will of the individual sinks into insignificance. That theory is, perhaps, not quite so common now as it was a few years ago. And surely, if any great event can be referred to the character of individual men, it was the crime of the seventeenth century in England, with its consequent train of evils. In that month of spring in the year 1603 when James Stuart was riding south to take up his crown in London, a prophetic eye might have foreseen the troubles he and his son were to cause. On the way the so-called Millenary Petition was presented to him by a band of moderate and conforming Puritans, who desired only a few unimportant changes in the service and Prayer Book; one of the first acts of James at Hampton Court was to deny the Petition and to abuse the petitioners with a threat to "harry them out of the land." After that the history of England for two generations was a series of *ifs*, depending on the actions of a small group of men. Thus, if Prince Henry, with his objection to a Catholic marriage, had not imprudently overheated himself on the tennis court, and so left the throne to his brother Charles; if Charles at the beginning of his reign had not been bribed to accept the Petition of Right and so to bind his hands; if Wentworth had been kept in England to raise a standing army, instead of being called back from Ireland when too late, and if Henrietta Maria by meddling with the soldiers had not brought him to the scaffold; if Charles had married a Protestant in-

stead of a Bourbon princess; if he had chosen a
wiser prelate than Laud; if he had not attempted
to seize the five members of Parliament, or had
planned the attempt more secretly; if the navy
had not been wantonly alienated; — If, in a
word, James and Charles had not been at once
so obstinate and so weak, either they might have
succeeded in establishing, for a time at least, a
monarchy like that raised in France on the ruin
of the Fronde and the Reformation, or they
might have guided their people through a blood-
less and healthy revolution. But for the fanaticism of the King the opposing fanaticism of Pym
and Lilburne and Cromwell would never have
come to the top, crushing between them the
moderate men who were the real strength and,
in the end, the salvation of England. And so I,
for one, cannot look back upon that period without shuddering at its passion of violent extremes,
and without a feeling of amazement that so much
evil in the world can be traced to the temper
of a few fanatics who, by the whim of Fortune,
had the destiny of the English people in their
hands.

Old England, though her richer and completer
development was perhaps forever marred by the
harsh divisions of that age, did nevertheless in a
manner quickly shake herself into balance. But
we must remember that the New England colonists, driven from their homes by the Laudian

persecution, came almost exclusively from one of
the national factions. They did not bring with
them the full temper of the English people, or
even that part of its character which has given
us Chaucer and Shakespeare and Dryden and
Swift and Johnson and Byron and Tennyson.
Their poetry therefore must be criticised, not as
belonging to the main current of English literature, but as a slender branch, so to speak, running to one side, and deprived of the broader
nourishment of tradition. It is the prolongation
of a mood that had been tortured into excess
by the goading stings of Accident; nor must we
forget that at home under the sway of this same
mood the imagination was distrusted, the the-
atres were closed, the picture collections of
Charles dispersed or destroyed, the churches
made barren of their beauty, the courtly poets
silenced or driven into obscure places — that the
land was for a time, in the language of Strafford,
"frequent in combustions, full of massacres and
the tragical ends of princes."

It would be unjust, of course, to say that
with this iconoclasm all the charm of life was
banished by the Puritans. Even leaving out of
account the supreme achievement of Milton,
no one can go through the writings of these men
without finding passages that have a grace entirely their own. One recalls, for instance, the
scene in Bunyan's pilgrimage, when Christian,

having twice climbed the Hill Difficulty, comes to the Palace Beautiful, and is there entertained by the maidens Piety, Prudence, and Charity. "Thus they discoursed together till late at night," the narrative proceeds, "and after they had committed themselves to their Lord for protection, they betook themselves to rest. The Pilgrim they laid in a large upper chamber, whose window opened towards the sunrising; the name of the chamber was Peace, where he slept till break of day; and then he awoke and sang." I shall not repeat the words of the Pilgrim's song, for Bunyan, with all his genius, endured the confinement of Bedford Gaol better than the shackles of rhyme; but no candid reader will fail to respond to the peculiar beauty of that chamber of peace. In this chastened loveliness, won by the exclusion of a whole half of life, the Puritan literature is not wanting. One foresees in it much that long afterwards will charm the ear in the poems of Longfellow and Whittier.

And in one respect the Puritans brought no diminution to the field of art and literature, but effected rather a return to the main line of tradition from which England for a while had been partially diverted by the seductions of the Renaissance. I mean that sense of something central and formative in man, of character as distinguished from the mere portrayal of unrelated passions, which was so lamentably lacking in most of the dramatists, and which since the advent of Puritanism has been the chief honour of British letters. With this subject I have already dealt at some length in the preceding series of these essays — as in fact I have touched here and there on the various other origins of the New England spirit — and need not repeat the argument; but it is highly important to remember this positive side of Puritanism when reckoning up the devastating effects of its rigid and combative morality on the imagination.

Now the very conditions of existence in New England exaggerated the seclusions of the half-civilization which the people brought over with them in their exile. Not only were the colonists withdrawn from contact with the secular tradition which makes itself so deeply felt in the art of a Milton, but the inevitable hardships of their state intensified their belief that life is a perpetual battle with the powers of evil, to whom no concession must be granted. In the dark unredeemed forests that surrounded them there lurked tribes of savage people whose appearance and habits were such as to warrant the notion that here indeed Satan was unchained and held undisputed sway. One of the first voyagers to the new continent, William Strachey, carried back this report of devil worship to credulous ears. "There is yet in Virginia," he wrote in 1618, "no place discovered so savadge and simple, in which the inhabitants have not a religion and the use of bow and arrows. All things they conceive able to do them hurt beyond their prevention, they adore with their kind of divine worship, as the fire, water, lightning, thunder, our ordinaunce pieces, horses, etc.; but their chief god they worship is no other, indeed, than the devill, whom they make presentments of, and shadow under the form of an idol, which they entitle Okeus." Naturally the settlers, looking out into the infinite wilderness, saw visions of dread and heard sounds of preternatural portent. Even the redoubtable Captain John Smith was sufficiently troubled to express his apprehensions in doggerel rhyme:

But his waking mind in hideous dreams did oft see wondrous shapes
Of bodies strange, and huge in growth, and of stupendous makes.

This may have been a passing sentiment in Virginia, but in Massachusetts it became a rooted conviction. It is the excuse, if any excuse be possible, for the wild delusion of witchcraft that for a time drove the leaders of Boston and Salem into a mania of fear and persecution. "The New Englanders," wrote Cotton Mather, "are a people of God settled in those which were once the devil's territories. . . . An army of devils is horribly broke in upon the place which is the centre and, after a sort, the first-born of our English settlements; and the houses of the good people there are fill'd with the doleful shrieks of their children and servants, tormented by invisible hands, with tortures altogether preternatural." If we were discussing the prose of America as well as the poetry, we should find in the after-effects of this superstition, this *deisidaimonia* in the true sense of the word, turned now from a religious conviction into a kind of haunting mood of the imagination, the sources of Hawthorne's dark psychology and no small part of that awe which Thoreau felt in the presence of the mountains and lonely forests.

Meanwhile we can see something of its influence in contracting the poetry of the colonists within still narrower bounds of religious sentiment. The first volume printed in this country was the Bay Psalm Book, translated from the Hebrew by Richard Mather, Thomas Welde, and John Eliot in 1640. In the preface Mather made this candid statement: "If therefore the verses are not alwaies so smooth and elegant as some may desire or expect, let them consider that God's altar needs not pollishings." And indeed the polishings are conspicuous by their absence, as any specimen of this notable book will show. For instance, the great nineteenth Psalm is thus rendered for the satisfaction of the faithful:

> The heavens doe declare
> The majesty of God:
> also the firmament shows forth
> his handy-work abroad.
> Day speaks to day, knowledge
> night hath to night declar'd.
> There neither speach nor language is
> where their voyce is not heard.

It would not be easy outside of Puritanism to find a great religion divesting itself so heroically not only of the smoothness and elegance but of the manifold traditions of life. But if the oracles of God were thus delivered through the nose, they could convey the menace of wrath as well as the upliftings of holiness. Perhaps the best known of the early New England poets is that Michael Wigglesworth who, for one fearless theological line, has obtained a kind of immortality in obloquy. Possibly a few of my readers will be unacquainted with Master Wigglesworth's picture of the terrors of the damned, when God at the Day of Doom has pronounced judgment upon them, and a merciful Christ has begun to consume the universe in fire:

> Then might you hear them rend and tear
> The air with their outcries;
> The hideous noise of their sad voice
> Ascendeth to the skies.
> They wring their hands, their caitiff-hands,
> And gnash their teeth for terror;
> They cry, they roar, for anguish sore,
> And gnaw their tongues for horror.

But get away without delay;
    Christ pities not your cry:
Depart to hell, there you may yell
    And roar eternally.

.   .   .   .

With iron bands they bind their hands
    And cursed feet together;
And cast them all, both great and small,
    Into that lake forever;
Where day and night, without respite,
    They wail and cry and howl,
For torturing pain which they sustain,
    In body and in soul.

For day and night, in their despite,
    Their torment's smoke ascendeth;
Their pain and grief have no relief,
    Their anguish never endeth.
There must they lie and never die,
    Though dying every day;
There must they, dying, ever lie,
    And not consume away.

Say what one will, there is a grim sincerity in
these lines which lifts them out of the commonplace and gives them something of the ring of
poetry; and after all, if you are going to depict
an eternal hell, there's no use in being finicky
about the benevolence of your deity. It is only
when our prophet of the New World vouchsafes
to make concessions to human sympathy that he
becomes odious. You know the words with which
the Almighty Judge is supposed to condemn the
little pleading souls of unbaptized infants:

You sinners are, and such a share
　　As sinners, may expect;
Such you shall have, for I do save
　　None but mine own elect.
Yet to compare your sin with their
　　Who lived a longer time,
I do confess yours is much less,
　　Though every sin's a crime.

A crime it is; therefore in bliss
　　You may not hope to dwell;
But unto you I shall allow
　　The easiest room in hell.

We shudder at that concession, "the easiest room in hell"; it really is odious. And yet, again, if we are to permit logic to deal with these matters, what possible difference does it make whether those chosen by God of His own free will for eternal damnation pass into this state after a few days of life or after many years? In either case their evil fate was imposed upon them at their birth. The only condemnation we can pronounce upon Wigglesworth is that, having allowed his natural human emotions to enter into the question at all, he stopped short halfway and did not revolt from the whole logical scheme of Calvinistic theology. I am disposed to feel a certain respect for this doggerel Dante of the New England meeting-house; though his power of expression was crude, there is in him, as in Jonathan Edwards and others of the line, an appalling energy and straightforwardness of the imagination. And if a late New Englander, Oliver Wendell Holmes, thought no decent man could really hold the doctrine of free grace and election without going mad, we must remember that Wigglesworth spoke the honest and deep-rooted conviction of his contemporaries — and they were not mad. And there is this, too, to be said for his unflinching sense of the awful consequences of sin, that it bears on the actual problems of life. One recalls that story of a farmer of the present day who was asked by a troubled clergyman why the village churches were left empty, and who replied with Yankee candour and shrewdness: "Wall, sir, I callate it is about like this: since you preachers have stopped preaching hell fire, we country folk have made up our minds that we might as well take our chances on t'other world."

But if the older theological taste had about it a prevailing odour of the pit, we must not infer that life in the colonies, gray in colour though it may have been, was entirely bleak and without those chambers towards the sunrise. Much of the verse produced may have been of the kind described by Captain Edward Johnson:

From silent night true Register of moans,
  From saddest soul consum'd in deepest sin,
From heart quite rent with sighs and heavy groans,
  My wailing muse her woful work begins,
And to the world brings tunes of sad lament,
Sounding naught else but sorrow's sad relent —

Much of the verse produced was of this nasal quality; but not all. Cotton Mather, he of the witchcraft fame, tells of a certain friend whose custom it was, "when he first arose in the morning, to repair into his study: a study well perfumed with the meditations and supplications of an holy soul." Can any scholar to-day hear that sentence without a thrill of envy at the thought of the long uninterrupted hours which those old divines contrived to pass in the earnest and unrepentant searching of mighty books? Ah, that study well perfumed with the meditations and supplications of an holy soul — how many a student of our age, distracted by the multitude of conflicting intellectual interests, disturbed by doubts of the value of learning in itself, when he enters his work-room of a morning, can breathe that atmosphere of assured content, as it were the palpable memory greeting him of similar days past? And this quiet satisfaction of a life devoted to retired scholarship and public teaching found due expression in literature. Nothing is more characteristic of the prose and poetry of the day than the innumerable eulogies of good men and women, to some of which the *pax theologica* lends an element of passionate sincerity. One of the best known of these is Urian Oakes's *Elegy on the Death of Thomas Shepard*, a saintly minister of Charlestown, who died in 1677. A few of the concluding stanzas will indicate the quality of the piece:

If to have solid judgment, pregnant parts,
A piercing wit, and comprehensive brain;
If to have gone the round of all the arts,
Immunity from death could gain; ...

If holy life, and deeds of charity,
If grace illustrious, and virtue tried,
If modest carriage, rare humility,
Could have bribed Death, good Shepard had not
   died. ...

. . . .

Farewell, dear Shepard! Thou art gone before,
Made free of heaven, where thou shalt sing loud hymns
Of high triumphant praises evermore,
In the sweet choir of saints and seraphims. ...

My dearest, inmost, bosom-friend is gone!
Gone is my sweet companion, soul's delight!
Now in an huddling crowd I'm all alone,
And almost could bid all the world — Good-night.
   Blest be my Rock! God lives; O let him be,
   As He is All, so All in All to me!

We need not magnify the virtues of such an
elegy as this, which would in fact appear poor
enough if compared with Milton's superb lines
on the reception of Edward King into the

   ... solemn troops, and sweet societies,
      That sing, and singing in their glory move,

or with Cowley's learned lament for his Cambridge companion in philosophy. Yet we shall
miss the truth if we fail to discover in Oakes's

less polished muse the charm of a friendship built upon a sure sympathy in the hopes of the spirit. As he himself wrote in one of the Latin verses whose elegance won the applause of his contemporaries,

Parvum parva decent, sed inest sua gratia parvis.

From these by-products of the theological laboratory we may turn aside to say something of the first and most ambitious of the professional poets of the age, the stupendous Anne Bradstreet, whose volume of verse was heralded to the world with this overwhelming title-page:

The Tenth Muse lately sprung up in America; or Several Poems, compiled with great variety of wit and learning, full of delight; wherein especially is contained a complete discourse and description of the four elements, constitutions, ages of man, seasons of the year; together with an exact epitome of the four monarchies, viz., the Assyrian, Persian, Grecian, Roman; also, a dialogue between Old England and New concerning the late troubles; with divers other pleasant and serious poems. By a gentlewoman in those parts. Printed at London, for Stephen Bowtell, at the sign of the Bible, in Pope's Head Alley, 1650.

Well, Mistress Anne was in sooth a memorable and characteristic figure of the New World. Though born and married in England, she migrated at the early age of eighteen to this country, and through her children became the fountain head of one of the purest streams of the so-

called Brahminism. One of her descendants was
Richard Henry Dana, another Oliver Wendell
Holmes. John Norton of Hingham, ancestor of
the present Nortons and Adamses, whose line
also was to intermarry with the Eliots, gave vent
to his admiration of the dead poetess in resounding couplets:

> Virtue ne'er dies: time will a poet raise,
> Born under better stars, shall sing thy praise.
> Praise her who list, yet he shall be a debtor;
> For Art ne'er feigned nor Nature framed, a better.
> Her virtues were so great, that they do raise
> A work to trouble fame, astonish praise.

I do not know that time has yet raised a poet
to celebrate her works to the taste of the pastor
of Hingham, but one of his descendants, the late
Charles Eliot Norton, edited the poems of the
matchless gentlewoman, and in his introduction
wrote of her character in his most genial vein.

All, indeed, that we know of Anne Bradstreet
from contemporary sources and from her own
autobiographical sketch justifies us in revering
her as one of those large-minded women of the
seventeenth century who managed somehow, in
ways that seem inexplicable to their daughters,
to combine the manifold cares of a household
with indefatigable study and sober unhurried
reflection. But the outpourings of her muse, it
must be acknowledged, remind us too forcibly of
one of her own aphorisms: "A ship that bears

much sail, and little or no ballast, is easily over-
set." She is seen perhaps at her best in such
stanzas as these:

I heard the merry grasshopper then sing,
  The black-clad cricket bear a second part,
They kept one tune, and played on the same string,
  Seeming to glory in their little art.
Shall creatures abject thus their voices raise?
And in their kind resound their Maker's praise:
Whilst I, as mute, can warble forth no higher lays.

. . . .

When I behold the heavens as in their prime,
  And then the earth (though old) still clad in green,
The stones and trees, insensible of time,
  Nor age nor wrinkle on their front are seen;
If winter come, and greenness then do fade,
A spring returns, and they more youthful made;
But man grows old, lies down, remains where once he's
    laid.

. . . .

O Time, the fatal wrack of mortal things,
  That draws oblivion's curtains over kings,
Their sumptuous monuments, men know them not,
  Their names without a record are forgot,
Their parts, their ports, their pomps all laid in th' dust,
Nor wit, nor gold, nor buildings 'scape time's rust;
But he whose name is grav'd in the white stone
Shall last and shine when all of these are gone.

Professor Barrett Wendell, who quotes these
stanzas, remarks aptly that in seventeenth-century New England the author "stands alone,
without forerunners or followers; and if you
compare her poetry with that of the old country,

you will find it very much like such then anti-quated work as the *Nosce Teipsum* of Sir John Davies, published in 1599, the year which gave us the final version of *Romeo and Juliet*." The female prodigy of New England, in fact, belongs to that strain of literary Puritanism which is more distinctly British than American, and which was already becoming outworn in the old home.

The names of Mrs. Bradstreet's more poetical descendants serve to remind us how intimately all this New England society was knit together, and how its spirit was handed down from generation to generation as a kind of family possession. Her own contemporary fame may call our attention to the fact that women played no inconsiderable part in creating the peculiar tone of the New World literature. And their influence was felt in two ways. In the first place that sturdiness and uprightness of character, which was one of the great, the very great, compensations of Puritanism, not only made itself heard in the eulogies pronounced over those who died in the harness of virtue, but was active in the family relations of the living. Saintliness, I know, does not invariably make for comfort. Sometimes the Puritan hardness of character dominated too tyrannically the softer traits of affection and compliance, bringing what might be called a desolation of sanctity into the home. But there were other households — and these I believe the majority — in which the tenderness to every duty, the sense of due subordination, the competence of training, the repose of a clear conscience, must have evoked an atmosphere of serene and equitable joy. The very discipline of the passions, the renunciation of the wider sweep of human experience, would put a stamp of sacredness on those chaster pleasures which knit a family together in contented unison. In a way all of New England may be said to have been snow-bound, in creed as well as in climate, but in the shelter of the hearth there was warmth for the body and there was comfort for the soul. Whittier was recalling a true incident of his childhood, and was writing also an allegory of New England's inner life, when he described that night of storm and snow:

> Shut in from all the world without,
> We sat the clean-winged hearth about,
> Content to let the north-wind roar
> In baffled rage at pane and door,
> While the red logs before us beat
> The frost-line back with tropic heat.

One can find in the older literature abundant evidence of these protected comforts of the home. Take for instance Cotton Mather's life of John Eliot. There, if anywhere, you have one of the stalwarts. So diligent was Eliot in study that he took to sleeping in his library, in order that he might get to his beloved books at some unearthly hour in the morning without disturbing the household. So fervid was he in piety that he is described as "perpetually 'jogging the wheel of prayer.'" Now the habit of perpetually jogging the wheel of prayer does not, I admit, sound alluring to our modern unsanctified ears; the appearance of a reverend jogger in our parlour would probably cause a little constraint, but then — other times other manners. And of Eliot we are assured by his biographer that "he was indeed sufficiently pleasant and witty in company, and he was affable and facetious in conversation." His affability, I doubt not, was only a part of the large charity of his nature. When an old man he said to one who questioned him about his state: "Alas, I have lost everything; my understanding leaves me, my memory fails me, my utterance fails me; but, I thank God, my *charity* holds out still; I find that rather grows than fails!" And his charity and affability, as well as his prayerfulness, were exercised at home, as sometimes in this strange world they are not. Of his relations with his wife it is said: "His whole conversation with her had that *sweetness*, and that *gravity* and *modesty* beautifying it, that every one called them Zachary and Elizabeth." The biographer continues: "God made her a rich blessing, not only to her *family*, but also to her *neighborhood;* and when she died,

I heard and saw her aged husband, who else very rarely wept, yet now with tears over the coffin, before the good people, a vast confluence of which were come to her funeral, say, 'Here lies my dear, faithful, pious, prudent, prayerful wife; I shall go to her, and she not return to me.'" These are the commonplaces of life, you may think, and perhaps they are, although I am not sure that peace and self-control are ever quite commonplace; but it is just these softer aspects of the old New England that we are likely to forget.

Now in the making of this home spirit the women naturally played an important rôle. Thomas Shepard, for example, he whose own elegy was sung so enthusiastically by Urian Oakes, had written a *Character of Mistress Joanna Shepard*, his wife, wherein he had portrayed her as "a woman of incomparable meekness of spirit, toward myself especially, and very loving; of great prudence to take care for and order my family affairs, being neither too lavish nor sordid in anything, so that I knew not what was under her hands. She had an excellency to reprove sin, and discern the evils of men." Incomparable meekness of spirit may not be precisely the sort of eulogy a modern wife would desire in her epitaph, however some husbands might desire it in her life — but, again, other times other manners. And if one is inclined to

shudder a little at the thought of her excellency
to reprove sin and discover the evils of men, one
may suspect that this sharp-edged knowledge
was useful in protecting her bookish and busy
husband from the inroads of fraudulent beggars
and evil mischief-makers. At any rate one may
be certain that the house of Mistress Joanna
Shepard much resembled the Palace Beautiful of
Bunyan, where the maidens Piety, Prudence,
and Charity kept watch and ward, and where
there was a large upper chamber of peace whose
window opened towards the sunrising. Certainly
also the peaceful affections of home, the cool and
quiet places of rest out of the turmoil of the
world's contentions, came to be a marked trait of
New England literature. There are traces of it
in the early poets; in the works of Whittier and
Longfellow it was to blossom into something
exceedingly precious, however it may lack the
more dazzling qualities of the imagination. The
other side of this truth is that you will find no
love poetry, as the word is commonly understood, in those primitive days — at least I know
of none — and there is a minimum of it in the
later age. That is an extraordinary fact, when
you stop to think of it, and to some may seem
a sad lack. Let such critics turn elsewhere;
heaven knows the erotic Muse has been vocal
enough in other sections of the world. For my
part I still prefer James Russell Lowell's *Under*

the Willows to the self-advertised passion of a certain living poetess who bears his family name.

That was one way in which the influence of women was felt. In another way they brought not peace but conflict into colonial life. The orthodoxy of the New England church was of a hard Calvinistic hue; it was eminently logical and intellectual, the creation and delight of strong men who, however they may have been possessed by a "boiling zeal" for saving souls, yet, like John Cotton, thought twelve hours of continuous study a "scholar's day" and true service to God. Against the virility, and one must add rigidity, of this religious dominion there were inevitably, almost from the beginning, movements of revolt. And it was natural that the good women of the colony should be conspicuous in rebellion as well as in meekness. Not all the great men of the land were as fortunate in their helpmates as were Thomas Shepard and John Eliot. In Winthrop's *History of New England from 1630 to 1649* there is an amusing story of one woman to whom much, and not a little, learning was a dangerous thing. "Mr. Hopkins, the governor of Hartford upon Connecticutt," we there read, "came to Boston, and brought his wife with him (a godly woman, and of special parts), who was fallen into a sad infirmity, the loss of her understanding and reason, which had been growing upon her divers

years, by reason of her giving herself wholly to
reading and writing, and had written many
books. Her husband, being very loving and
tender of her, was loath to grieve her; but he
saw his error, when it was too late. For if she
had attended her household affairs, and such
things as belong to women, and not gone out of
her way and calling to meddle in such things as
are proper to men, whose minds are stronger,
etc., she had kept her wits." I do not know by
what stages this learned lady fell into her sad
infirmity, but I suspect she betook herself to
her books as a refuge from her spouse, the
worthy governor, of whom it is related "that he
frequently fell a bleeding at the nose, through
the agony of spirit with which he laboured in
them [his prayers]." Neither do I know what
was in her many books — even the all-embracing
Tyler does not mention them — but my guess
is that she wrote verse and tampered with the
man-made mysteries of religion.

At least this second form of audacity was
what brought trouble between another "godly
woman" and the rulers of the State. The story
of the conflict may be read in Thomas Welde's
Heresies of Anne Hutchinson, from which it
would appear that this strong-minded female
had the pious, and in those days obligatory,
habit of going regularly to meeting, but added
the very bad habit of collecting a company of

critical folk after service and of expounding to them the sermon in a spirit of contumely and contradiction. Now the colonists had a high sense of the value of liberty, as was natural in men who had suffered so much in its cause — so high a sense that, in the words of Governor Winthrop, they would have it only "maintained and exercised in a way of subjection to authority." But this was not the view of Anne Hutchinson and her coterie. Liberty to them meant the freedom of the individual, not to follow the truth, but to choose the truth; it was the kind described by Winthrop as making "men grow more evil, and in time to be worse than brute beasts: *omnes sumus licentia deteriores*," and as "that great enemy of truth and peace, that wild beast, which all the ordinances of God are bent against, to restrain and subdue it."

We will not now enter into the question of truth as it lay between the preachers of the Commonwealth and Mistress Hutchinson, but there is no doubt of the fact that her manner of prophesying did not bring peace. The result of her lectures among the women is thus denounced by Thomas Welde:

Now, oh their boldness, pride, insolency, alienations from their old and dearest friends, the disturbances, divisions, contentions they raised amongst us, both in church and State, and in families, setting division between husband and wife!...

Now the faithful ministers of Christ must have dung cast on their faces, and be no better than legal preachers, Baal's priests, popish factors, scribes, Pharisees, and opposers of Christ himself.

And it was not only against the persons of the clergy that Anne Hutchinson lifted her terrible prophetic voice; she struck at the very dogmatic centre of their authority. She lays a profane hand on the intellectual and traditional basis of theology; — as the horrified author of the *Wonder-Working Providence* exclaimed: she is a "woman that preaches better than any of your black-coats that have been at the Ninneversity." Her heresy is analysed at length by Thomas Welde, but it is really summed up in the single charge: "This witness of the Spirit is merely immediate, without any respect to the word, or any concurrence with it." That is to say, she was sent into exile for teaching exactly what two centuries afterwards was to be the doctrine of Emerson's essays and Whittier's most exquisite work. Her proclamation of the witness speaking in the breast of each man, and requiring no confirmation from revealed book or ordained interpreter, was a signal of the course to be pursued by her people, starting with rebellion against institutions and rites and ending in rejection of all authority and tradition and the very principle of organization. She was the first, and remains the typical, "come-outer."

Lowell remembered these passages at arms when, in his *Biglow Papers*, he described the troubles caused by the townswomen of the good pastor of Jaalam:

The painful divisions in the First Parish, A.D. 1844, occasioned by the wild notions of (what Mr. Wilbur, so far as concerned the reasoning faculty, always called) the unfairer part of creation, put forth by Miss Parthenia Almira Fitz, are too well known to need more than a passing allusion. It was during these heats, long since happily allayed, that Mr. Wilbur remarked that "the Church had more trouble in dealing with one *she*resiarch than with twenty *he*resiarchs," and that the men's *conscia recti*, or certainty of being right, was nothing to the women's.

It is a pity, I often think, that Lowell, who could have translated Cotton Mather into puns without depriving him of his Puritan savour, lived too early to try a fling at New England's latest *she*resiarch — the feminine counterpart of Emerson's refusal to face the reality of evil in the world.

It remained for Whittier, who as a Quaker found it easier to give free expression to the inner voice which had supplanted the religion of reason, to do justice, or more than justice, to those feminine flails of the man-made church. Often in his ballads Whittier makes use of the heresies that filled the early divines with terror, as if in prospect of the coming dissolution of

their iron-bound creeds. And it is the women of
Boston who are chiefly remembered by him for
introducing the leaven of rebellion. Cassandra
Southwick, who was threatened with exile and
slavery for entertaining Quakers and neglecting
divine service, is one of his heroines. Another
is Margaret Brewster, who suffered worse than
threatenings for coming into the South Church
barefoot and in sackcloth, and crying out against
the rulers and magistrates of the town.

> She shook the dust from her naked feet,
>   And her sackcloth closer drew,
> And into the porch of the awe-hushed church,
>   She passed like a ghost from view.
>
> They whipped her away at the tail o' the cart
>   Through half the streets of the town,
> But the words she uttered that day nor fire
>   Could burn nor water drown.
>
> And now the aisles of the ancient church
>   By equal feet are trod,
> And the bell that swings in its belfry rings
>   Freedom to worship God!

So did the spirit and poetry of early New
England become an inheritance; out of the
strong was to come sweetness, out of the un-
couth grace. It will be objected, I fear, that in
my treatment of the subject I have said much
of the spirit and little of the poetry of the age;
but in truth poets in those days were something

like the historian's snakes in Ireland: there were n't any. As the first satirist, and not the worst, of the colony, Nathaniel Ward, the Simple Cobbler of Agawam, declared:

> Poetry's a gift wherein but few excel,
> He doth very ill, that doth not passing well.

Enough has been quoted from the primitive verse-makers to show that none of them did passing well; but enough also has been said, I trust, to show that some acquaintance with their spirit is a profitable, almost a necessary, preparation for approaching that fine and ephemeral thing, the flowering of New England in the first half of the nineteenth century.

It is rather the fashion, I am aware, among a certain coterie of enlightened critics to condemn the later poetry of New England as almost equally negligible with that of the men and women we have been considering. And indeed no rightly informed person will rank the outpourings of Concord and Cambridge with the supreme creations of the older centres of civilization. We are not likely to fall into that error of over-praise; but we may be tempted by the clamour of our emancipated youth, hailing largely from strange lands in the dark map of Europe, to miss the more fragile beauty of what after all is the fairest thing this country has produced. At its best the poetry of New England

is one of the very desirable possessions of the
world, and not to appreciate it is to prove one's
self dulled and vulgarized by the strident conceit
of modernity. It is limited no doubt, and for
reasons which I have tried to set forth. But
limitation is not always and altogether a vice.
At least out of the limitations fixed by the origin
of New England grew the peculiar attitude of
the later writers towards nature, the charm of
their portrayal of the less passionate affections
of the home and the family, the absence of erotic
appeal, the depth and sincerity, but the perilous
independence also, of their religious intuition,
the invincible rightness of their character. We
may laugh as we will at old Wigglesworth and
at the asthmatic Muse of the other Puritan divines; they have been justified of their children.

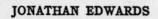

JONATHAN EDWARDS

JONATHAN EDWARDS

JONATHAN EDWARDS was born at Windsor, Connecticut, in 1703. He belonged, unlike his great
contemporary Franklin in this, to the "Brahmin
families" of America, his father being a distinguished graduate of Harvard and a minister
of high standing, his mother being the daughter
of Solomon Stoddard, the revered pastor of
Northampton, Massachusetts, and a religious
author of repute. Jonathan, one of eleven children, showed extraordinary precocity. There is
preserved a letter of his, written apparently in
his twelfth year, in which he retorts upon the
materialistic opinions of his correspondent with
an easiness of banter not common to a boy; and
another document, from about the same period,
an elaborate account of the habits of spiders,
displays a keenness of observation and a vividness of style uncommon at any age. He who
could write such a sentence as the following was
already a master in his own right: "In very calm
and serene days in the forementioned time of
year, standing at some distance behind the end
of an house or some other opaque body, so as
just to hide the disk of the sun and keep off his
dazzling rays, and looking along close by the
side of it, I have seen a vast multitude of little

shining webs, and glistening strings, brightly reflecting the sunbeams, and some of them of great length, and of such a height that one would think they were tacked to the vault of the heavens, and would be burnt like tow in the sun."

He studied at Yale, receiving his bachelor's degree in 1720, before his seventeenth birthday. While at college he continued his interest in scientific observations, but his main concern was naturally with theology and moral philosophy. As a sophomore he read Locke *On the Human Understanding*, with the delight of a "greedy miser" in "some newly discovered treasure." Some time after reading Locke and before graduation he wrote down a series of reflections, preparatory to a great metaphysical treatise of his own, which can only be compared with the *Commonplace Book* kept by Berkeley a few years earlier for the same purpose. In the section of *Notes on the Mind* this entry is found: "Our perceptions or ideas, that we passively receive by our bodies, are communicated to us immediately by God." Now Berkeley's *Principles* and his *Hylas and Philonous* appeared in 1710 and 1713 respectively, and the question has been raised, and not answered, whether this Berkeleian sentiment was borrowed from one of these books or was original with Edwards. Possibly the youthful philosopher was following a line of thought suggested by the English disciples of Male-branche, possibly he reached his point of view directly from Locke; in any case his life work was to carry on the Lockian philosophy from the point where the Berkeleian idealism left off.

After graduation Edwards remained for two years at Yale, preparing for the ministry. In 1722 he was called to a Presbyterian church in New York. Here he preached acceptably for eight months, returning then to his father's house, and later to New Haven, where he held the position of tutor in the college. In 1727 he went to Northampton as colleague, becoming in due time successor, to his grandfather. Almost immediately after ordination he married Sarah Pierrepont, like himself of the Brahmin caste, whom he had known as a young girl, and whose beauty of body and soul he had described in a passage of ecstatic wonder. "They say," he be-gan, being himself then twenty and the object of his adoration thirteen, "there is a young lady in New Haven who is beloved of that great Be-ing who made and rules the world, and that there are certain seasons in which this great Being, in some way or other invisible, comes to her and fills her mind with exceeding sweet delight." The marriage, notwithstanding this romantic rapture, proved eminently wise. Lying on his deathbed at Princeton, while his wife was far away in Northampton, he could, after a life not

without sore trials and difficulties, send her this
message: "Tell her that the uncommon union
which has so long subsisted between us, has been
of such a nature as I trust is spiritual, and therefore will continue forever." They had eleven
children, one of whom married the Reverend
Aaron Burr, president of Nassau Hall (now
Princeton University), and was the mother of a
more famous son of the same name.

Like a good many other men of his age Edwards lived his inner life, so to speak, on paper —
a custom which may seem morbid to a generation taught to believe that it is better to look
out than to look in, but which has the advantage
of counteracting the disruptive work of time and
of linking the periods of life together into one
conscious whole. There is therefore nothing
peculiar or priggish in the fact that at the beginning of his religious career he should have
written out a set of formal resolutions, which he
vowed to read over, and did read over, at stated
intervals in order to keep watch on his spiritual
progress. A number of these resolutions have
been printed, as has also a part of the diary kept
at about the same time. Neither of these documents, the time of their writing considered, contains anything remarkable, unless our knowledge
of the author's life justifies us in attaching unusual significance to such words as the following,
which in themselves might have been set down

by a thousand other young men of the age: "I have been to God this morning, and told him that I gave myself *wholly* to him."

But it is quite otherwise with the private reflections which he wrote out some twenty years later (about 1743) at Northampton, apparently on some occasion of reading over his youthful diary. In this we have an autobiographical fragment that, for intensity of absorption in the idea of God and for convincing power of utterance, can be likened to the *Confessions* of St. Augustine, while it unites to this religious fervour a romantic feeling for nature foreign to the Bishop of Hippo's mind and prophetic of a movement that was to sweep over the world many years after Edwards' death. A few extracts from this document (not so well known as it would have been if not printed with the works of a thorny metaphysician) must be given for their biographical and literary interest:

From my childhood up, my mind had been full of objections against the doctrine of God's sovereignty, in choosing whom he would to eternal life, and rejecting whom he pleased; leaving them eternally to perish, and be everlastingly tormented in hell. It used to appear like a horrible doctrine to me. But I remember the time very well, when I seemed to be convinced, and fully satisfied, as to this sovereignty of God.... I have often, since that first conviction, had quite another kind of sense of God's sovereignty than I had then. I have often since had not only a conviction, but a delightful conviction. The doctrine has very often appeared exceedingly pleasant, bright, and sweet. Absolute sovereignty is what I love to ascribe to God. But my first conviction was not so.

The first instance that I remember of that sort of inward, sweet delight in God and divine things that I have lived much in since, was on reading those words, *Now unto the King eternal, immortal, invisible, the only wise God, be honour and glory for ever and ever, Amen.* As I read the words, there came into my soul, and was as it were diffused through it, a sense of the glory of the Divine Being.

Not long after I first began to experience these things, I gave an account to my father of some things that had passed in my mind. I was pretty much affected by the discourse we had together; and when the discourse was ended, I walked abroad alone, in a solitary place in my father's pasture, for contemplation. And as I was walking there, and looking up on the sky and clouds, there came into my mind so sweet a sense of the glorious *majesty* and *grace* of God, that I know not how to express. I seemed to see them both in a sweet conjunction; majesty and meekness joined together; it was a sweet and gentle, and holy majesty; and also a majestic meekness; an awful sweetness; a high, and great, and holy gentleness.

God's excellency, his wisdom, his purity and love, seemed to appear in everything; in the sun, and moon, and stars; in the clouds and blue sky; in the grass, flowers, trees; in the water, and all nature; which used greatly to fix my mind. I often used to sit and view the moon for continuance; and in the day spent much time in viewing the clouds and sky, to behold the sweet glory of God in these things; in the mean time, singing forth, with a low voice, my contemplations of the Creator and Redeemer.

I spent most of my time in thinking of divine things, year after year; often walking alone in the woods, and solitary places, for meditation, soliloquy, and prayer, and converse with God.

Holiness, as I then wrote down some of my contemplations on it, appeared to me to be of a sweet, pleasant, charming, serene, calm nature; which brought an inexpressible purity, brightness, peacefulness and ravishment to the soul. In other words, that it made the soul like a field or garden of God, with all manner of pleasant flowers; all pleasant, delightful, and undisturbed; enjoying a sweet calm, and the gentle vivifying beams of the sun. The soul of a true Christian, as I then wrote my meditations, appeared like such a little white flower as we see in the spring of the year; low and humble on the ground, opening its bosom to receive the pleasant beams of the sun's glory; rejoicing as it were in a calm rapture; diffusing around a sweet fragrancy; standing peacefully and lovingly, in the midst of other flowers round about.

This is not the Edwards that is commonly known, and indeed he put little of this personal rapture of holiness into his published works, which were almost exclusively polemical in design. Only once, perhaps, did he adequately display this aspect of his thought to the public; and that was in the *Dissertation on the Nature of Virtue*, wherein, starting from the definition of virtue as "the beauty of the qualities and exercises of the heart," he proceeds to combine ethics and æsthetics in an argument as subtle in reasoning as it is, in places, victorious in expression. One cannot avoid the feeling when his

writings are surveyed as a whole, despite the
laxness of his style, that in his service to a particular dogma of religion Edwards deliberately
threw away the opportunity of making for himself one of the very great names in literature.

It should seem also that he not only suppressed
his personal ecstasy in his works for the press, but
waived it largely in his more direct intercourse
with men. He who himself, like an earlier and
perhaps greater Emerson, was enjoying the
sweetness of walking with God in the garden of
earth, was much addicted to holding up before his
people the "pleasant, bright, and sweet" doctrine of damnation. Nor can it be denied that he
had startling ways of impressing this sweetness
on others. It is a misfortune, but one for which
he is himself responsible, that his memory in the
popular mind to-day is almost exclusively associated with certain brimstone sermons and their
terrific effect. Best known of these is the discourse on *Sinners in the Hands of an Angry God*,
delivered at Enfield, Connecticut, in the year
1741. His text was taken from Deuteronomy:
"Their foot shall slide in due time"; and from
these words he proceeded to prove, and "im-
prove," the truth that "there is nothing that
keeps wicked men at any moment out of hell, but
the mere pleasure of God." He is said to have
had none of the common qualities of the orator.
His regular manner of preaching, at least in his

earlier years, was to hold his "manuscript volume in his left hand, the elbow resting on the cushion or the Bible, his right hand rarely raised but to turn the leaves, and his person almost motionless"; but there needed no gesticulation and no modulation of voice to convey the force of his terrible conviction, when, to an audience already disposed to accept the dogma, he presented that dogma in a series of pictures beside which the Inferno of Dante seems like the naïveté of a child:

How awful are those words, Isaiah lxiii, 3, which are the words of the great God: "I will tread them in mine anger, and trample them in my fury, and their blood shall be sprinkled upon my garments, and I will stain all my raiment." It is perhaps impossible to conceive of words that carry in them greater manifestations of these three things, viz., contempt and hatred, and fierceness of indignation. If you cry to God to pity you, he will be so far from pitying you in your doleful case, or showing you the least regard or favour, that instead of that he will only tread you under foot: and though he will know that you cannot bear the weight of omnipotence treading upon you, yet he will not regard that, but he will crush you under his feet without mercy; he will crush out your blood, and make it fly, and it shall be sprinkled on his garments, so as to stain all his raiment. He will not only hate you, but he will have you in the utmost contempt; no place shall be thought fit for you but under his feet, to be trodden down as the mire in the streets.

There is reason to think, that there are many in this congregation now hearing this discourse, that will actually be the subjects of this very misery to all eternity. We know not who they are, or in what seats they sit, or what thoughts they now have. It may be they are now at ease, and hear all these things without much disturbance, and are now flattering themselves that they are not the persons; promising themselves that they shall escape. If we knew that there was one person, and but one, in the whole congregation, that was to be the subject of this misery, what an awful thing it would be to think of! If we knew who it was, what an awful sight it would be to see such a person! How might all the rest of the congregation lift up a lamentable and bitter cry over him! But alas! Instead of one, how many is it likely will remember this discourse in hell! And it would be a wonder, if some that are now present should not be in hell in a very short time, before this year is out. And it would be no wonder if some persons, that now sit here in some seats of this meeting-house in health, and quiet and secure, should be there before to-morrow morning.

The congregation of Enfield, we are told, was moved almost to despair; "there was such a breathing of distress and weeping" that the speaker was interrupted and had to plead for silence. Sincerity of vision may amount to cruelty, and something is due to the weakness of human nature. Dr. Allen, the biographer of Edwards, is right in saying that "he was almost too great a man to let loose upon other men in their ordinary condition. He was like some organ of vast capacity whose strongest stops or combinations should never have been drawn."

The result was inevitable. Life is made up of

ordinary men in their ordinary condition. The people of Northampton listened to Edwards for a time; were rapt out of themselves; suffered the relapse of natural indolence; grew resentful under the efforts to keep them in a state of exaltation; and freed themselves of the burden when it became intolerable. That, in brief, is the explanation of the difference between Edwards and the people of his parish, ending in his dismissal from Northampton. So at least it would be if we judged from the contemporary point of view; from another point of view it may be described as the certain outcome of a combat between inhuman logic and common sense.

At first all went well. Mr. Stoddard, in whose declining years the discipline of the church had been somewhat relaxed, died in 1729, and the fervour of his successor soon began to tell on the people. In 1733, as Edwards notes in his *Narrative of Surprising Conversions*, there was a stirring in the conscience of the young, who had hitherto been prone to the awful sin of "frolicking." The next year the sudden conversion of a young woman, "who had been one of the greatest company keepers in the whole town," came upon the community "like a flash of lightning"; the Great Awakening was started, which was to run over New England like a burning fire, with consequences not yet obliterated. The usual accompaniments of moral exaltation and physical convulsions showed themselves. Edwards relates with entire approbation the morbid conversion of a child of four. The poor little thing was overheard by her mother in her closet wrestling with God in prayer, from which she came out crying aloud and "wreathing her body to and fro like one in anguish of spirit." She was afraid she was going to hell! And so, "she continued thus earnestly crying and taking on for some time, till at length she suddenly ceased crying and began to smile, and presently said with a smiling countenance — Mother, the kingdom of heaven is come to me!" This was the beginning of "a very remarkable abiding change in the child"; thereafter she loved "to hear Mr. Edwards preach," delighted in religious conversations, and had "a great concern for the good of other souls." Like saints of an older age she could not always distinguish between rapture and despair:

At some time about the middle of winter, very late in the night, when all were in bed, her mother perceived that she was awake, and heard her as though she was weeping. She called to her, and asked her what was the matter. She answered with a low voice, so that her mother could not hear what she said; but thinking it might be occasioned by some spiritual affection, said no more to her; but perceived her to lie awake, and to continue in the same frame for a considerable time. The next morning she asked her whether she did not cry the last night: the child answered yes, I did cry a little, for I was thinking about God and Christ, and they loved me. Her mother asked her, whether to think of God and Christ's loving her made her cry: she answered yes, it does sometimes.

It was inevitable that such a wave of super-heated emotion should subside in a short time. In fact the enthusiasm had scarcely reached its height when it began to show signs of indubitable perversion, and decay. Immediately after the story of the young convert Edwards notes that "the Spirit of God was gradually withdrawing" and "Satan seemed to be let loose and raged in a dreadful manner." An epidemic of melancholy and suicidal mania swept over the community, and multitudes seemed to hear a voice saying to them: "Cut your own throat, now is a good opportunity." Strange delusions arose and spread, until common sense once more got the upper hand.

It was an old tale, told in New England with peculiar fury. The saddest thing in the whole affair is the part played by Edwards. Other leaders saw the danger from the first, or were soon aroused to it; but Edwards never, either at this time or later, wavered in his belief that the Awakening, though marred by the devil, was in itself the work of the Divine Spirit. His *Thoughts on the Survival of Religion* and his *Marks of a Work of the True Spirit* are both a thoroughgoing apology for the movement, as they are also an important document in his own psychology. The

jangling and confusion he admits; he recognizes
the elements of hysteria that were almost in-
extricably mixed up with the moral exaltation of
conversion; but his defence is based frankly on
the avowal that these things are the universal
accompaniments of inspiration — they attended
the founding of the church in the Apostolic age,
they were to be expected at the reinstauration
of religion. Often the reader of these treatises is
struck by a curious, and by no means accidental,
resemblance between the position of Edwards
and the position of the apologists of the romantic
movement in literature. There is the same directness of appeal to the emotions; the same lauda-
tion of expansiveness, at the cost, if need be, of
judgment or measure or any other restraint.
Prudence and regularity may be desirable in the
service of God, yet it is still true that "the
cry of irregularity and imprudence" has been
chiefly in the mouths of those who are enemies
to the main work of redemption. Perturbation,
in truth, is not properly so called when it is the
means of rousing the cold and indifferent from
their lethargy; we are bound to suppose that not
even the man "of the strongest reason and
greatest learning" can remain master of himself
if "strongly impressed with a sense of divine and
eternal things." And thus the religious apologist
rises into the equivalent of "Titanism": "When
God is about to bring to pass something great

and glorious in the world, nature is in a ferment and struggle, and the world as it were in travail." It comes in the end to this, that, notwithstanding his verbal reservations, Edwards had no critical canon to distinguish between the order and harmony governed by a power higher than the tumultuous sway of the emotions and the order and harmony that are merely stagnation.

One factor in his confidence was a belief that the discovery of America, coinciding as it did with the beginning of the Reformation, came by Providence for "the glorious renovation of the world"; nay more, that the humble town in which he was preaching might be the cradle of the new dispensation, from whence it should spread over the whole earth. His language may even seem to betray a touch of spiritual pride over the part he himself should be called upon to play as the instrument of Grace in this marvellous regeneration. That vice of the saints was indeed a subject much in his meditations, and one of the finest pieces of religious psychology in his works is the passage of the *Revival* in which he tracks it through the labyrinthine deceits of the human heart. Pride no doubt was a sin against which he had to keep particular ward in these years, but we should not say that he ever, in any proper sense of the word, lapsed from the virtue of Christian humility. If he seemed to set himself

above other men as an exigent judge, this was
rather due to a faulty sympathy, an inability to
measure others except by the standard of his
own great faculties. Thus, for all his emotionalism, he lived under the control of an iron will,
and he could not comprehend how the over-
stimulation of terror and joy in a weaker disposition would work moral havoc. Nor from his
own constant height could he understand how
brief and fitful any mood of exaltation must be
among ordinary men in their ordinary condition.
Hence he not only failed to see the gravity of the
actual evils at the time of the Awakening, but
failed also, with more grievous results for himself, to recognize the impossibility of flogging the
dead emotion into new life.

The issue came on a point of church discipline.
Edwards believed that religion was essentially a
matter of the emotions, or affections. A man
might have perfect knowledge of divine things,
as indeed the devil had, but unless the love of
God was implanted in his heart by the free act of
Grace he had no lot with the faithful. To develop this theme he wrote his great *Treatise Concerning Religious Affections*, a work which without exaggeration may be said to go as far as the
human intellect can go in the perilous path of
discriminating between the purely spiritual life
and the life of worldly morality. The hard kernel of the argument is stated thus:

From these things it is evident, that those gracious influences which the saints are subjects of, and the affects of God's Spirit which they experience, are entirely above nature, altogether of a different kind from any thing that men find within themselves by nature, or only in the exercise of natural principles; and are things which no improvement of those qualifications, or principles that are natural, no advancing or exalting them to higher degrees, and no kind of composition of them, will ever bring men to; because they not only differ from what is natural, and from every thing that natural men experience, in degree and circumstances, but also in kind; and are of a nature vastly more excellent. And this is what I mean, by supernatural, when I say that gracious affections are from those influences that are supernatural.

From hence it follows, that in those gracious exercises and affections which are wrought in the minds of the saints, through the saving influences of the Spirit of God, there is a new inward perception or sensation of their minds, entirely different in its nature and kind....

...And even in those things that seem to be common, there is something peculiar; both spiritual and natural love cause desires after the object beloved; but they be not the same sort of desires: there is a sensation of soul in the spiritual desires of one that loves God, which is entirely different from all natural desires: both spiritual love and natural love are attended with delight in the object beloved; but the sensations of delight are not the same, but entirely and exceedingly diverse. Natural men may have conceptions of many things about spiritual affections; but there is something in them which is as it were the nucleus, or kernel of them, that they have no more conception of, than one born blind, has of colours. 4653

Now even this simple statement of the difference between the condition of Grace and the
condition of nature is hard for the natural man
to follow; but when Edwards, with the acumen
of a genius and the doggedness of a scholar, imposed his distinction on all the intricate feelings
of life, the natural man was dazed; and when he
attempted to make it the criterion of admission
to the Lord's Table, the natural man who
called himself a Christian rebelled. Stoddard
had thought it right to admit to communion all
those who desired honestly to unite themselves
with the church. Edwards protested that only
those who had undergone a radical conversion
and knew the affections of supernatural love
should enjoy this high privilege. His congregation sided with their old guide against him.

The quarrel was further embittered by another
issue. It came to light that certain young folk
of the church were reading profane books which
led to lewd conversation. Edwards called for
public discipline of the sinners; the congregation
supported him until investigation showed that
the evil was widespread and would bring discredit on most of the better families of the town,
and then they blocked further proceedings. If
tradition is correct in naming *Pamela* as one of
the guilty books, we may admire the literary
taste of youthful Northampton, yet think that
their pastor was justified in condemning such

reading as incendiary. However that may be, when, on the 22nd of June, 1750, a public vote was taken whether Mr. Edwards should be dismissed from his pastorate, a large majority was counted against him. Northampton has the distinction of having rejected the greatest theologian and philosopher yet produced in this country. As Socrates taunted the ancient politicians for the injuries they suffered at the hands of those they were supposed to have trained in civic virtue, so perhaps the townsmen of Edwards might retort upon any accuser that, if they failed in religious duty, it was the business of their pastor to have instructed them more effectively.

The behaviour of Edwards when the crisis actually came was simple, dignified, and even noble. His *Farewell Sermon*, with its dispassionate and submissive appeal from the tribunal of men to that final judgment which shall be given in knowledge and righteousness, cannot be read to-day without a deep stirring of the heart: "And let us all remember, and never forget our future solemn meeting on that great day of the Lord; the day of infallible decision, and of the everlasting and unalterable sentence. Amen."

At the age of forty-six Edwards was thrust upon the world, discredited, in broken health, with a large family to support, undaunted. Then befell a strange thing. This philosopher,

whose thoughts and emotions ranged beyond the
ken of most educated men, was sent to the fron-
tier town of Stockbridge as a missionary to the
Indians. There for six years he laboured faithfully
and, at least in the practical management of
affairs, successfully. It must have been one of
the memorable sights of the world to have seen
him returning on horseback from a solitary ride
into the forest, while there fluttered about him,
pinned to his coat, the strips of paper on which
he had scribbled the results of his meditations.
His days were little troubled, and not over-
burdened with work, peaceful it is thought; and
now it was he wrote the treatise on the *Freedom of the Will* upon which his fame chiefly depends.

In 1757 his son-in-law died, and Edwards was
chosen by the Trustees of the College of New
Jersey to succeed him as president. Edwards
hesitated, stating frankly to the Trustees his dis-
abilities of health and learning; but finally accepted the offer. He left his family to follow him
later, and arrived in Princeton in January of
1758. Small-pox was in the town and the new
president was soon infected. His death took
place on the 22nd of March, in the fifty-fourth
year of his age. His last recorded words were:
"Trust in God and ye need not fear."

The child was indeed father of the man, and it
was peculiarly fitting that he who from youth

upward had been absorbed in the idea of God should have died with the sacred word on his lips. But what shall be said of the fearlessness of one who had made terror the chief instrument of appeal to men and had spent his life in fighting for a dogma which the genial author of *The One-Hoss Shay* thought no decent man could hold without going crazy?

Now the Edwardian theology was a part of the great deistic debate which took its root in the everlasting question of the origin of evil in the world. It was a three-cornered contest. The Calvinists and the infidels both believed in a kind of determinism, but differed over the nature of the determining cause. The Calvinists found this cause in a personal Creator, omnipotent and omniscient, to whom they did not scruple to carry up all the evil as well as the good of the universe — "c'est que Dieu," as Calvin himself states categorically, "non seulement a preveu la cheute du premier homme, et en icelle la ruine de toute sa posterité, mais qu'il l'a ainsi voulu." The Deists, who at this time formed the fighting line of the infidels, while verbally acknowledging the existence of God and theorizing on the nature of evil, virtually regarded the universe as a perfectly working machine in which there was no room for a personal governor or for real sin. To the Arminians, including the bulk of the orthodox Churchmen, the alliance between

Calvinism and Deism seemed altogether to out-
weigh the differences. As Daniel Whitby declares in the preface to his discourses *On the Five
Points of Calvinism*, to hold God responsible for
evil is to play directly into the hands of the
atheists. And so the age-old dispute between
Augustinian and Pelagian, and between Calvin-
ist and Arminian, took on a new life from the
deistic controversy, and there sprang up a literature which undertook to preserve the idea of
an omnipotent personal Creator and at the same
time to save His face, if the expression may be
tolerated, by attributing to man complete free
will and accountability for his actions. Dr.
Whitby, whose discourses appeared in 1710 (re-
printed in America), was a man of considerable
learning but of no great metaphysical acumen,
and a writer, as one of his critics said, of "dis-
gusting tautology." His argument consists
mainly in heaping up quotations from the philosophers and early Fathers, typical of which are
these two, chosen with cunning application to
his opponents from St. Augustine himself: "It
is the height of madness and injustice to hold
any person guilty because he did not that which
he could not do," and "Who will not pronounce
it folly to command him who is not free to do
what is commanded?" The clear moral inference
follows: God does punish men, therefore they
have in themselves the power to live righteously;

and God does command and exhort men, therefore their will is free to obey or disobey.

It was in answer to Whitby's book and one or two others of the kind that Edwards composed his *Freedom of the Will*. His argument has a psychological basis. In the *Treatise Concerning Religious Affections* he had divided the soul into two faculties: one the understanding, by which it discerns, views, and judges things; the other called the heart or will, being nothing else but the inclination of the soul towards, or the disinclination from, what is discerned and judged by the understanding. In the *Freedom of the Will* he starts with Locke's statement that "the Will is perfectly distinguished from Desire, which in the very same action may have a quite contrary tendency from that which our Wills set us upon." This theory Edwards analyses and rejects, and then proceeds to show that a man's desire and will are virtually the same faculty of the soul. It follows from this that the will at any moment is determined by the strongest motive acting upon the soul; we are free in so far as no obstacle is presented to our willing in accordance with our inclination, but our inclination is determined by what at any moment seems to us good. In his attack on the common arguments for the freedom of the will Edwards is magnificently victorious. If the psychology by which the Arminians sought to relieve God of the burden of evil in human life

is pushed into a corner, it shows itself as nothing
more than this: Man's will is a faculty absolutely
indeterminate in itself and entirely independent
of his inclinations. When, therefore, a man errs,
it is because, the choice between evil with its
attendant suffering and good with its attendant
happiness being presented to him, the man,
having full knowledge of the consequences and
being impelled by no momentary preponderance
of the one or the other from his innate disposition, deliberately and freely chooses what is evil
and painful. Such an account of human action
is monstrous, inconceivable; it offered an easy
mark for so sharp a logician as Edwards.

But whence arise the conditions by which a
man's inclination is swayed in one direction or
the other? Edwards carries these unflinchingly up
to the first cause, that is, as a Christian, to God.
Berkeley had made the world to consist of ideas
evoked in the mind of man by the mind of God;
Edwards accepts the logical conclusion, and holds
God responsible for the inclination of the human
will which depends on these ideas. To the charge
that such a theory makes God the author of evil
he replies in these terms:

If, by *the author of sin*, is meant the permitter, or
not a hinderer of sin; and, at the same time, a disposer
of the state of events, in such a manner, for wise, holy,
and most excellent ends and purposes, that sin, if it
be permitted or not hindered, will most certainly and

infallibly follow: I say, if this be all that is meant, by being the author of sin, I do not deny that God is the author of sin (though I dislike and reject the phrase, as that which by use and custom is apt to carry another sense). . . . This is not to be the *actor of sin*, but, on the contrary, *of holiness.*

Calvin, as we have seen, did not hesitate to attribute the source of evil to God's will in franker words than these, but at the same time he warned men against intruding with their finite reason into this "sanctuary of the divine wisdom." The mind of Edwards could not rest while any problem seemed to him unsolved. Confronted with the mystery of the divine will, he undertakes to solve it by applying his psychology of man to the nature of God. (He himself would put it the other way about: "Herein does very much consist that image of God wherein He made man.") The passage in which he most explicitly develops this thesis, though generally overlooked by his critics, is of the first importance:

We must conceive of Him as influenced in the highest degree, by that which, above all others, is properly a moral inducement, viz., the moral good which He sees in such and such things: and therefore He is, in the most proper sense, a moral Agent, the source of all moral ability and Agency, the fountain and rule of all virtue and moral good; though by reason of his being supreme over all, it is not possible He should be under the influence of law or command, promises or threatenings, rewards or punishments, counsels or warnings. The essential qualities of a moral Agent are in God, in the greatest possible perfection; such as understanding, to perceive the difference between moral good and evil; a capacity of discerning that moral worthiness and demerit, by which some things are praiseworthy, others deserving of blame and punishment; and also a capacity of choice, and choice guided by understanding, and a power of acting according to his choice or pleasure, and being capable of doing those things which are in the highest sense praiseworthy.

In other words, the will of God is precisely like the will of man; it is merely the inclination, or *moral inducement*, to act as He is *influenced* by an external power. The fatal mystery of good and evil, the true cause, lies somewhere above and beyond Him; He is, like ourselves, a channel, not the source. The only difference is that God has complete knowledge of the possibilities of being, and therefore is not moved by threats and blind commands, but immediately, by what Edwards elsewhere calls the "moral necessity" of governing in accordance with the best of the "different objects of choice that are proposed to the Divine Understanding." By such a scheme God is really placed in about such a position as in the Leibnitzian continuation of Laurentius Valla's *Dialogue on Free Will and Providence*, where He is naïvely portrayed as looking upon an infinite variety of worlds piled up, like cannon balls, in pyramidal form before Him, and selecting for creation that one which combines the greatest possible amount of good with the least possible admixture of evil.

From this pretty sport of the imagination Edwards would no doubt have drawn back in contempt, and, indeed, in his ordinary language God is merely the supreme Cause, without further speculation. One of the Leibnitzian inferences, moreover, is utterly excluded from his philosophy. He was no optimist; was in fact the last man to infer that, because this world is the best possible conceivable, evil is therefore a small and virtually negligible part of existence. On the contrary the whole animus of his teaching springs from a deep and immediate hatred of evil in itself and apart from any consideration of its cause. "The thing," he says, "which makes sin hateful, is that by which it deserves punishment; which is but the expression of hatred. . . . Thus, for instance, ingratitude is hateful and worthy of dispraise, according to common sense; not because something as bad, or worse than ingratitude, was the cause that produced it; but because it is hateful in itself, by its own inherent deformity."

To the charge of the Arminians that the doctrine of predestination leaves no place for the punishment of sin, this is an adequate reply; but the consequences are, in another way, disastrous to the Edwardian theology. If we are right, as we indubitably are right, in detesting

evil in itself and wherever seen, and if we hold
with Edwards that the will of God, like the will
of man, is merely the inclination towards the
best object presented to its choice, and there is
no power either in God or in man above the
will, in what essential way, then, does the act
of God in creating a world mixed with evil differ from the act of Judas in betraying God, and
how are we relieved from hating God for the
evil of His work with the same sort of hatred
as that which we feel for Judas? Edwards had
terrified the people of Enfield with a picture of
God treading down sinners till their blood
sprinkled His raiment, and exulting in His
wrath. The retort is obvious, and unspeakable.
Nor can he, or any other Predestinarian, escape
the odium of such a retort by hiding behind
the necessity of things which all men must, in
one way or another, admit. There is a war between the nations, he will say, and suddenly a
bomb, dropping upon a group of soldiers, themselves innocent of any crime, horribly rends
and mangles them. Here is a hideous thing, and
by no twisting of the reason can you or I avoid
carrying the responsibility for this evil back to
the first great cause of all. Shall I be held im-
pious for saying metaphorically that the blood
of these soldiers is sprinkled on the raiment of
that Cause? — Aye, but the difference to us
morally if we leave that cause in its own vast

obscurity, unapproached by our reason, untouched by our pride; or if we make it into an image of ourselves, composed only of understanding and inclination like our own, and subject to our reprobation as surely as to our love!

Edwards had riddled and forever destroyed the arguments for free will commonly employed by the Arminians; is there no alternative for the human reason save submission to his theological determinism or to fatalistic atheism?

One way of escape from that dilemma is obvious and well known. It is that which Dr. Johnson, with his superb faculty of common sense, seized upon when the Edwardian doctrine came up in conversation before him. "The only relief I had was to forget it," said Boswell, who had read the book; and Johnson closed the discussion with his epigram: "All theory is against the freedom of the will, all experience for it." That is sufficient, no doubt, for the conduct of life; yet there is perhaps another way of escape, which, if it does not entirely silence the metaphysical difficulties, at least gives them a new ethical turn. Twice in the course of his argument Edwards refers to an unnamed Arminian[1] who

---

[1] Edwards, it should seem, had immediately in mind the *Essay on the Freedom of Will in God and the Creature* of Isaac Watts; but the notion had been discussed at length by Locke (*Essay* II, XXI), and at an earlier date had been touched on with great acumen by John Norris in his correspondence with Henry More.

placed the liberty of the soul not in the will itself,
but in some power of suspending volition until
due time has elapsed for judging properly the
various motives to action. His reply is that this
suspension of activity, being itself an act of volition, merely throws back, without annulling, the
difficulty; and as the argument came to him, this
refutation is fairly complete. But a fuller consideration of the point at issue might possibly
indicate a way out of the dilemma of free will
and determinism into a morally satisfying form
of dualism within the soul of man himself.[1] At
least it can be said that the looseness of the
Arminian reasoning leaves an easier loophole of
escape into a human philosophy than does the
rigid logic of the Predestinarians.

Yet for all that, though we may follow Edwards' logical system to the breaking point, as
we can follow every metaphysical system, and
though we may feel that, in his revulsion from
the optimism of the Deists, he distorted the
actual evil of existence into a nightmare of the
imagination, — yet for all that, he remains one
of the giants of the intellect and one of the endur-
ing masters of religious emotion. He had not the
legal and executive brain of Calvin, upon whose
Institutes his scheme of theology is manifestly
based, but in subtle resourcefulness of reasoning
and still more in the scope of his spiritual in-

[1] This argument is developed in my *Platonism*, 127 ff.

sight he stands, I think, above his predecessor. Few men have studied Edwards without recognizing the force and honesty of his genius. To Hazlitt he ranked with Hobbes, Berkeley, Butler, Hartley, Hume, and Leibnitz as a metaphysician. To Crabb Robinson the reading of his book on *Original Sin*, in early youth, was "an irreparable mischief." Let us take our leave of him with one of his more gracious meditations impressed on our memory:

All the truly great and good, all the pure and holy and excellent from this world, and it may be from every part of the universe, are constantly tending toward heaven. As the streams tend to the ocean, so all these are tending to the great ocean of infinite purity and bliss.

EMERSON

EMERSON

It becomes more and more apparent that Emerson, judged by an international or even by a true national standard, is the outstanding figure of American letters. As a steady force in the transmutation of life into ideas and as an authority in the direction of life itself he has obtained a recognition such as no other of his countrymen can claim. And he owes this preeminence not only to his personal endowment of genius, but to the fact also that, as the most complete exponent of a transient experiment in civilization, he stands for something that the world is not likely to let die.

Ralph Waldo Emerson, born in Boston, May 25, 1803, gathered into himself the very quintessence of what has been called the Brahminism of New England, as transmitted through the Bulkeleys, the Blisses, the Moodys, and the direct paternal line. Peter Bulkeley, preferring the wilderness of Satan to Laudian conformity, came to this country and, in 1636, founded Concord. William Emerson, his descendant in the fifth generation, was builder of the Old Manse in the same town, and a sturdy preacher to the minute-men at the beginning of the Revolution; and of many other ministerial ancestors stories abound which show how deeply implanted in this stock was the pride of rebellion against traditional forms and institutions, united with a determination to force all mankind to worship God in the spirit. With William, son of him of Concord and father of our poet, the fires of zeal began to wane. Though the faithful pastor of the First Church (Unitarian) of Boston, it is recorded of him that he entered the ministry against his will. Yet he too had his unfulfilled dream of "coming out" by establishing a church in Washington which should require no sort of profession of faith. He died when the future philosopher was a boy of ten, leaving the family to shift for itself as best it could. Mrs. Emerson cared for the material welfare of the household by taking in boarders. The chief intellectual guidance fell to the aunt, Mary Moody Emerson, of whom her nephew drew a portrait in his *Lectures and Biographies.* "She gave high counsels," he says. Indubitably she did; but a perusal of her letters and the extracts from her journals leaves the impression that the pure but erratic enthusiasms of her mind served rather to push Emerson in the direction of his weaker inclination than to fortify him against himself. When a balloon is tugging at its moorings there is need of low counsels.

In 1817, Emerson entered Harvard College, and in due course of time graduated. Then, after

teaching for a while in his brother's school in
Boston, he returned to Cambridge to study for
the ministry, and was in the autumn of 1826
licensed to preach. Three years later he was
called to the Second Church of Boston, as
assistant to Henry Ware, whom he soon succeeded. His ministration there was quietly successful, but brief. In 1832, he gave up his charge
on the ground that he could not conscientiously
celebrate the Communion, even in the symbolic
form customary among the Unitarians. He was
for the moment much adrift, his occupation
gone, his health broken, his wife lost after a
short period of happiness. In this state he went
abroad to travel in Italy, France, and England.
One memorable incident of the journey must be
recorded, his visit to Carlyle at Craigenputtock,
with all that it entailed of friendship and influence; but beyond that he returned with little
more baggage than he took with him. He now
made his residence in Concord, and married a
second wife, who was to be a true helpmeet until
the end. Thenceforth there was to be no radical
change in his life, but only the gradual widening
of the circle. The house that he bought, he continued to inhabit until it was burned down in
1872; and then his friends, in a manner showing
exemplary tact, subscribed money for rebuilding
it on the same lines. For a number of years he
preached in various pulpits, and once even con-

sidered the call to a settled charge in New Bedford, but could not overcome his aversion to the ritual of the Lord's Supper and to regular prayers.

Meanwhile, by the medium of lectures delivered here and there and by printed essays, he was making of himself a kind of lay preacher to the world. His method of working out the more characteristic of these discourses has long been known. He would select a theme, and then ransack his note-books for pertinent passages which could be strung together with the addition of such developing and connecting material as was necessary. But since the publication of his *Journals* it has been possible to follow him more precisely in this procedure and to see more clearly how it conforms with the inmost structure of his mind. These remarkable records were begun in early youth and continued, though at the close in the form of brief memoranda, to the end of his life. The first entry preserved (not the first written, for it is from *Blotting Book*, No. XVII) dates from his junior year at college and contains notes for a prize dissertation on the Character of Socrates. Among the sentences is this:

What is God? said the disciples, and Plato replied, It is hard to learn and impossible to divulge.

And the last page of the record, in the twelfth volume, repeats what is really the same thought:

The best part of truth is certainly that which hovers in gleams and suggestions unpossessed before man. His recorded knowledge is dead and cold. But this chorus of thoughts and hopes, these dawning truths, like great stars just lifting themselves into his horizon, they are his future, and console him for the ridiculous brevity and meanness of his civic life.

There is of course much variety of matter in the *Journals* — shrewd observations on men and books, chronicles of the day's events, etc. — but through it all runs this thread of self-communion, the poetry, it might be called, of the New England conscience deprived of its concrete deity and buoying itself on gleams and suggestions of eternal beauty and holiness. Of the same stuff, not seldom indeed in the same words, are those essays of his that have deeply counted; they are but a repetition to the world of fragments of this long inner conversation. Where they fail to reach the reader's heart, it is not so much because they are fundamentally disjointed, as if made up of sentences jostled together like so many mutually repellent particles; as because from the manner of his composition Emerson often missed what is the essence of good rhetoric, that is to say the consciousness of his hearer's mind as well as of his own. We hear him as it were talking to himself, with no attempt to convince by argument or to enlighten by analysis. If our dormant intuition answers to his, we are profoundly kindled and confirmed; otherwise his sentences may rattle ineffectually about our ears.

Emerson's first published work was *Nature* (1836), which contains the gist of his transcendental attitude towards the phenomenal world, as a kind of beautiful symbol of the inner spiritual life floating dreamlike before the eye, yet, it is to be noted, having discipline as one of its lessons for the attentive soul. The most characteristic and influential of his books are the two volumes of *Essays*, issued respectively in 1841 and 1844. In the former of these are those great discourses on Self-Reliance, Compensation, and the Over-Soul, into which was distilled the very quintessence of the volatile and heady liquid known as Emersonianism. Other volumes followed in due course. The later publications, however, beginning with *Letters and Social Aims* (1875), are made up mainly of gleanings from the field already harvested, and were even gathered by hands not his own.

Two of his addresses (now both included in the volume with *Nature*) deserve special notice for the attention they attracted at the time. The first of these is the oration before the Phi Beta Kappa Society of Harvard, in 1837, a high but scarcely practical appeal to the American Scholar to raise himself above the dust of pedantries, even out of the routine of what is "decent, indolent, complaisant," and to reach

after the inspiration of "the Divine Soul which
also inspires all men." The other lecture was
delivered the next year before the senior class in
Divinity College, Cambridge, and held up to the
prospective preacher about the same ideal as
was presented to the scholar. Historical Christianity is condemned because "it is not the
doctrine of the soul, but an exaggeration of the
personal, the positive, the ritual. It has dwelt,
it dwells, with noxious exaggeration about the
person of Jesus." The founder of Christianity
saw, indeed, "with open eye the mystery of the
soul," but what as a man he saw and knew of
man's divinity cannot be given to man to-day
by instruction, but only on the terms of a like
intuition. The Unitarians of Massachusetts had
travelled far from the Calvinistic creed of the
Pilgrim Fathers, but Emerson's suave displace-
ment of the person of Jesus for the "chorus of
thought and hopes" in any human soul, perhaps
even more his implicit rejection of all rites and
institutions, raised a good deal of protest among
the worshippers of the day. For the most part
he answered the criticism by silence, but in a
letter replying to one of the more courteous of
his opponents he used these significant words:
"I could not give an account of myself, if chal-
lenged. I could not possibly give you one of the
'arguments' you cruelly hint at, on which any
doctrine of mine stands; for I do not know what

arguments are in reference to any expression of a thought." There may be some guile in this pretence to complete intellectual innocence, but it is nevertheless a fair statement of a literary method which seeks, and obtains, its effect by throwing a direct light into the soul of the hearer and bidding him look there and acknowledge what he sees.

Of the events of these years there is not much to relate. A journey to Europe, in 1847, resulted in the only two of his books that may be said to have been composed as units: *Representative Men* (published in 1850, from a series of lectures delivered in London), which displays Emerson's great powers as an ethical critic, and *English Traits* (1856), which proves that his eyes were observing the world about him with Yankee shrewdness all the while that he seemed to be gazing into transcendental clouds. Into the question of slavery and disunion which was now agitating the country, he entered slowly. It was natural that one to whom the power and meaning of institutions had little appeal and to whom liberty was the all-including virtue, should have been drawn to the side of the Abolitionists, but at first there was a philosophical aloofness in his attitude. Only after the passing of the Fugitive Slave Law and Webster's defection were his passions deeply engaged. Then he spoke ringing words:

There is infamy in the air. I have a new experience. I awake in the morning with a painful sensation, which I carry about all day, and which, when traced home, is the odious remembrance of that ignominy which has fallen on Massachusetts, which robs the landscape of beauty, and takes the sunshine out of every hour.

And the war came to him as a welcome relief from a situation which had grown intolerable.

A third trip to Europe was made in 1872, when his central will was already relaxing and his faculties were losing their edge. It was at this time that Charles Eliot Norton talked with Carlyle, and heard the old man, eight years older than Emerson, expatiate on the fundamental difference in their tempers. Norton records the conversation in his Journal:

As we were sitting together just after my coming in this afternoon, Carlyle spoke of Emerson. "There's a great contrast between Emerson and myself. He seems verra content with life, and takes much satisfaction in the world, especially in your country. One would suppose to hear him that ye had no troubles there, and no share in the darkness that hangs over these old lands. It's a verra strikin' and curious spectacle to behold a man so confidently cheerful as Emerson in these days.

"Well, it may be as you say. I'm not such a verra bloody-minded old villain after all," (here a cordial laugh,) "not quite so horrid an ogre as some good people imagine. But the warld is verra black to me; and I see nothin' to be content with in this brand new, patent society of ours."

For some time there had been a gradual loosening of Emerson's hold on life. Though always an approachable man and fond of conversation, there was in him a certain lack of human warmth, of "bottom," to use his own word, which he recognized and deplored. Commenting in his *Journal* (May 24, 1864) on the burial of Hawthorne, he notes the statement of James Freeman Clarke that the novelist had "shown a sympathy with the crime in our nature," and adds: "I thought there was a tragic element in the event, that might be more fully rendered, — in the painful solitude of the man, which, I suppose, could not longer be endured, and he died of it." A touch of this romantic isolation, though never morose or "painful," there was in himself, a failure to knit himself strongly into the bonds of society. "I have felt sure of him," he says of Hawthorne in the same passage, "in his neighbourhood, and in his necessities of sympathy and intelligence, — that I could well wait his time, — his unwillingness and caprice, — and might one day conquer a friendship. . . . Now it appears that I waited too long." Eighteen years later, standing by the body of Longfellow, he was heard to say: "That gentleman was a sweet, beautiful soul, but I have entirely forgotten his name." Such forgetfulness, like a serene and hazy cloud, hovered over Emerson's brain in his closing years. A month afterwards, on the 27th of April, 1882, he himself faded away peacefully.

He lies buried under the shadow of a tall pine-tree in Sleepy Hollow.

To one who examines the events of Emerson's quiet life with a view to their spiritual bearing it will appear that his most decisive act was the surrender of his pulpit in 1832. Nearly a century earlier, in 1750, the greatest of American theologians had suffered what now befell the purest of American seers; and though the manner of their parting was different (Jonathan Edwards had been unwillingly ejected, whereas Emerson left with good will on both sides), yet there is significance in the fact that the cause of separation in both cases was the administration of the Lord's Supper. Nor is there less significance in the altered attitude of the later man towards this vital question. Both in a way turned from the ritualistic and traditional use of the Communion, and in this showed themselves leaders of the spirit which had carried the New England Fathers across the ocean as rebels against the Laudian tyranny of institutions. Edwards had revolted against the practice of Communion as a mere act of acquiescence in the authority of religion; he was determined that only those should approach the Table who could give evidence of a true conversion, by conversion meaning a complete emotional realization of the dogma of divine Grace and election. The eucharist was not a rite by conforming with which in humility men were to be made participators in the larger religious experience of the race, but a jealously guarded privilege of the few who already knew themselves set apart from the world. He was attempting to push to its logical issue the Puritan notion of religion as a matter of individual and inward experience; and if he failed it was because life can never be rigidly logical and because the worshippers of his day were already beginning to lose their intellectual grasp on the Calvinistic creed. By Emerson's time, among the Unitarians of Boston, there could be no question of ritualistic grace or absolute conversion, but his act, nevertheless, like that of Edwards, was the intrusion of unyielding consistency among those who were content to rest in habit and compromise.

Emerson had come to the inevitable conclusion of New England individualism; he had, in a word, "come out." Edwards had denied the communal efficacy, so to speak, of rites, but had insisted on inner conformity with an established creed. Emerson disavowed even a conformity in faith, demanding in its stead the entire liberty of each soul to rise on its own spiritual impulse. He was perspicacious and honest enough to acknowledge to himself the danger of such a stand. "I know very well," he wrote in his journal at the time of his decision, "that it is a bad sign in a man to be too conscientious, and stick at gnats.

The most desperate scoundrels have been the
over-refiners. Without accommodation society
is impracticable." But, he adds, he could "not
go habitually to an institution which they esteem
holiest with indifference and dislike"; and again,
looking deeper into his heart, "This is the end of
my opposition, that I am not interested in it."

Emerson's act of renunciation was not only
important as determining the nature of his career, but significant also of the transition of New
England from theological dogmatism to romantic
liberty. Much has been written about the influences that shaped his thoughts and about the relation of his transcendentalism to German meta-
physics. In his later years it is clear that the
speculations of Kant and Schelling and Fichte
were known to him and occasionally coloured his
language, but his *Journals* prove conclusively
enough that the whole stamp of his mind was
taken before these sources were open to him.
Indirectly, no doubt, something of the German
spirit came to him pretty early through Carlyle,
and a passage in his *Journal* for December 13,
1829, shows that he was at that time already
deeply engaged in the Teutonized rhapsodies of
Coleridge. But it would be easy to lay too much
stress even on this indirect affiliation. Long before that date, as early as his senior year in college, he is yearning "to separate the soul for sublime contemplation till it has lost the sense of cir-

cumstances," and otherwise giving implicit expression to the full circle of transcendental faith. He was in fact the product of a great movement that was sweeping over the world as it listed; his early reading went back mainly to the Greek philosophers and the poets and preachers of seventeenth-century England, but they were interpreted by him under the light of the new emancipation of the emotions. When he declared, in *Nature*, that "the vision of genius comes by renouncing the too officious activity of the understanding, and giving leave and amplest privilege to the spontaneous sentiment," he was merely stating in precise terms an idea familiar to Blake and to the romanticists of every land — the elevation of enthusiasm above judgment, of emotion above reason, of spontaneity above discipline, and of unlimited expansion above centripetal control. But there was another element as strongly formative of Emerson's disposition as was the broadening current of rebellion against the reason, and that was his ancestral inheritance. Romantic spontaneity moved in various directions in accordance with the field in which it worked; in an Emerson, with all the divinity of Massachusetts in his veins, it might move to repudiate theological dogma and deny Jehovah, but it could not get out of hearing of the question "What is God?" It could not fall into the too common confusion of spiritual aspiration with the sicklier lusts of the flesh; it could never, for all its centrifugal wandering, overstep the bounds of character. There, I think, we touch the quick of the matter. The course of Puritan emancipation led in the end to an individualism and a trust in sheer unrestrained spontaneity which are in many ways akin to the temper of the European revolt. You will find the marks of this affiliation as far back as in the reveries in which Jonathan Edwards records his isolation from mankind and absorption in inanimate nature; and when German literature reached this land it found in Emerson and Longfellow and others a material ready to its hand. But with all the similarity between the two movements and despite the influence of German literature, when it came, upon Concord and Cambridge, there remained this striking and fundamental distinction: the spontaneity and individualism of the romantic movement on the Continent went with a dissolution of character against which the Puritan mind, so long as it held true to its origin, was impregnably fortified. Emersonianism may be defined as romanticism rooted in Puritan divinity.

It is scarcely necessary to illustrate this union of religious individualism and stability of character by quotations from Emerson's verse; yet, for the light they throw on his literary method, if for no other reason, I will quote one or two of his

familiar pieces. The best known expression of
the idea of the deity sitting in the breast of each
man, yet embracing the world, is found in those
stanzas entitled *Brahma*, which, it is hard to
know why, caused such a stir when they first
appeared. Even clearer in purport, as showing
how this faith in the inner power grew out of the
Puritan distrust of traditional rites and institutions, are the opening lines of *The Problem:*

> I like a church; I like a cowl;
> I love a prophet of the soul;
> And on my heart monastic aisles
> Fall like sweet strains, or pensive smiles:
> Yet not for all his faith can see
> Would I that cowlèd churchman be.
>
> Why should the vest on him allure,
> Which I could not on me endure?
> Not from a vein of shallow thought
> His awful Jove young Phidias brought;
> Never from lips of cunning fell
> The thrilling Delphic oracle;
> Out from the heart of nature rolled
> The burdens of the Bible old;
> The litanies of nations came,
> Like the volcano's tongue of flame,
> Up from the burning core below, —
> The canticles of love and woe:
> The hand that rounded Peter's dome
> And groined the aisles of Christian Rome
> Wrought in a sad sincerity;
> Himself from God he could not free;
> He builded better than he knew; —
> The conscious stone to beauty grew.

It is significant of this confidence in individual inspiration that generally in Emerson, as in other poets, it tends to looseness and formless spontaneity of style. When, on the contrary, he turns to the note of character, his language becomes instantly terse and restrained, and falls naturally into symmetrical form. Matthew Arnold has cited for approval the two quatrains in which this note is heard most clearly:

> So nigh is grandeur to our dust,
> So near is God to man,
> When Duty whispers low, *Thou must*,
> The youth replies, *I can* —

and this other,

> Though love repine and reason chafe,
> There came a voice without reply, —
> "'T is man's perdition to be safe,
> When for the truth he ought to die."

(It may be interesting to observe that the two last lines, as we learn from Emerson's *Journal*, were taken bodily from the sermon of a Puritan divine preached in 1642. That by the way.) Of the two quatrains as a whole Matthew Arnold remarks that they are "exceptional" in our poet. They are that, and something more: they are exceptional in literature. One would have to search far in English to discover anything equal to them in their own kind. They have the cleanness and radiance of the couplets of the Greek Simonides. They may look easy, but as a matter of fact the ethical epigram is an extremely difficult *genre*, and to attain this union of gravity and simplicity is one of the supreme accomplishments of art. Along with absolute sureness of touch there is required an entire balance and control of the faculties, a deep respect for the springs of human nature — in a word character.

While speaking of these traits I ought not to pass by the little poem entitled *Days*, in which the feeling for beauty in itself, superadded to insight and the note of character, produces a work of exquisite finish and haunting charm:

Daughters of Time, the hypocritic Days,
Muffled and dumb like barefoot dervishes,
And marching single in an endless file,
Bring diadems and fagots in their hands.
To each they offer gifts after his will,
Bread, kingdoms, stars, and sky that holds them all.
I, in my pleachèd garden, watched the pomp,
Forgot my morning wishes, hastily
Took a few herbs and apples, and the Day
Turned and departed silent. I, too late,
Under her solemn fillet saw the scorn.

These, it must be admitted, are rare occurrences in Emerson, the event of what Plato would call a divine chance; if they had come oftener, or had been at his command, he would have been, despite the limitations of his subject-matter, one of the very great poets of the world. But this was not to be. On the contrary, by the side of these poems which are marked by mas-

terly form and restraint you will find others, and
these the more numerous, in which he surrenders
himself to the shifting breath of inspiration like a
rudderless boat, to such a degree, indeed, that
over much of his work his own word "whim"
might be set as a superscription.

The philosophy of his prose essays — so far as
he can be said to have systematized his thoughts
at all — shows this same light-hearted legerde-
main. Nor is this philosophy hard to discover;
the whole circle of his ideas is likely to be present,
explicit or implicit, in any one of his great passages: — the clear call to self-reliance, announc-
ing that "a man should learn to detect and watch
that gleam of light which flashes across his mind
from within"; the firm assurance that, through
all the balanced play of circumstance, "there is a
deeper fact in the soul than compensation, to wit,
its own nature"; the intuition, despite all the
mists of illusion, of the Over-Soul which is above
us and still ourselves: "We live in succession, in
division, in parts, in particles; meanwhile within
man is the soul of the whole; the wise silence; the
universal beauty. . .; the eternal One."

Emerson's philosophy is thus a kind of vanish-
ing dualism, and a man's attitude towards it in
the end will be determined by his sense of its
sufficiency or insufficiency to meet the facts of
experience. One of Emerson's latest biographers
has attempted to set forth this philosophy as "a

synthesis and an anticipation," in that we find in it, as Emerson had already found in Plato and Plotinus, a reconciliation which all men are seeking of "the many and the one," the everlasting flux and the motionless calm at the heart of things:

An ample and generous recognition of this transiency and slipperiness both in the nature of things and in man's soul seems more and more a necessary ingredient in any estimate of the universe which shall satisfy the intellect of the coming man. But it seems equally true that the coming man who shall resolve our problems will never content himself with a universe a-tilt, a universe in cascade, so to speak; the craving for permanence in some form cannot be jauntily evaded. Is there any known mind which foreshadows the desired combination so clearly as Emerson's? Who has felt more profoundly the evanescence and evasiveness of things? ... Yet Emerson was quite as firm in his insistence on a single unalterable reality as in his refusal to believe that any aspect or estimate of that reality could be final.[1]

The necessity of the dualism that underlies Emerson's philosophy could scarcely be put more neatly, and the kind of synthesis, or reconciliation, in which Emerson floated is admirably expressed. But I am not so sure that this synthesis anticipates the solution of the troublesome problems of life, or that it will afford the kind of spiritual consolation which hitherto mankind has found in religion. There will be those who will

[1] O. W. Firkins, *Ralph Waldo Emerson*, 364.

ask whether the power of religion for mature minds does not depend after all on its feeling for evil as a tremendous reality? How otherwise, in fact, shall religion meet those harder questions of experience when its aid is most needed? And in like manner they will say that the power of philosophy as the *dux vitæ* depends on its acquaintance with the scope and difficulties of scepticism? Both religion and philosophy would seem, in such a view, to rest not only on a statement of the dualism of good and evil, knowledge and ignorance, but on a realization of the full meaning and gravity, practical and intellectual, of this dualism. Now Emerson certainly recognizes the double nature of experience, but it is a fair question whether he realizes its full meaning and fateful seriousness. He accepts it a trifle too jauntily; is sometimes too ready to wave aside its consequences, as if a statement of the fact were an escape from its terrible perplexities. To be reconciled so cheerfully to this dark dilemma is not a reconciliation of the dilemma itself, but argues rather some deep-lying limitation of spiritual experience. Carlyle meant something of the sort when he worried over Emerson's inability to see the hand of the devil in human affairs — a strange paradoxical charge to bring against the purest inheritor of the old faith of New England, yet essentially true.

A good way to learn what this denial of evil

led to in practice is to turn from Emerson to some of his weaker-minded followers or friends. For example, Bronson Alcott, one of the Concord illuminati, chanced to be in England in the year 1842, and there, in concert with one or two Englishmen who had imbibed his vaporous ideas, concocted a plan to found in the vicinity of Boston and Concord "a New Eden," where man might live in primitive simplicity and forget the wretched illusion of the existence of sin. So came about the experiment of "Fruitlands," the communal farm of philosophers at the village of Harvard, one of the funniest and, for some of those involved, one of the saddest attempts to disregard the facts of life and human nature.

Of the group of "consecrated cranks," as a rebel afterwards styled them, one, a mild lunatic named Samuel Brown, believed in salvation by the grace of nakedness. The poor fellow soon became discontented because, in deference to the ladies of the community, they forced him to restrict his practice of salvation to the hours of night, and even then to mitigate its purity by wearing a single garment. In that garb he used to wander over the hills like a white ghost, until rumours of the unearthly apparition got about among the farming folk and caused a prosaic search for the visitant with a *posse comitatis*. Meanwhile, as he was confined to his chamber by day, he did not contribute much to the physical well-being

of the settlement. Another of the genial come-
outers was a cooper by trade, described in a letter
as "an excellent assistant here, very faithful to
every work he undertakes, very serious." That
sounds promising. But unfortunately there were
drawbacks to his full acceptance by the leaders
of the band. He "has had rather deep experience," continues the writer of the letter, "having
been imprisoned in a mad house by his relatives
because he had a little property, but still he is not
a spiritual being, at least not consciously and wish-
fully so." Really that is one of the most delicious
sentences on record from the pen of a saint —
imprisoned in a mad house, but still (note the conjunction) not a spiritual being.

These good people had a double purpose: one,
sufficiently humble, to support themselves, that
is their unmentionable bodies, on the pure fruits
of the earth; the other, more elevated, to plant "a
love colony," as their Eden was called, where the
brotherhood of man should reign unpolluted by
the lust of property, and by their illustrious example to aid "entire human regeneration." It
cannot be said that they succeeded very well in
feeding themselves, and when food was bad they
took it out, like other mortals, in grumbling at
the cooks. The men of the colony were so absorbed in the contemplation of the mystery of
holiness that the fruits of the field rather lan-
guished. As Alcott's daughter said, they "were

so busy discussing and defining great duties that they forgot to perform the small ones." The barley crops somehow would not harvest themselves, so they were got in by the women while the masculine sages were wandering off in the amiable desire of "aiding entire human regeneration." Things grew worse and worse, until it came to a question of leaving or starving. It is very pretty to declare that the body is "all sham"; but you can't feed it by shamming work.

And as for the spirit, by some unaccountable means the serpent seems to have crept into this Eden, as he did into the original experiment. The "love colony" soon developed into a circle of disappointed, jealous, fault-finding men and women, who found it to their advantage to seek shelter from one another by scattering in the wicked world. This is one of Father Hecker's memoranda: "Somebody once described 'Fruitlands' as a place where Mr. Alcott looked benign and talked philosophy, while Mrs. Alcott and the children did all the work." It is well to look benign, but another of the colonists wrote in a different vein. "All the persons," he complains, "who have joined us during the summer have from some cause or other quitted, they say in consequence of Mr. Alcott's despotic manner, which he interprets as their not being equal to the Spirit's demands." It looks a little as if these spiritual demands were not unaccompanied with

spiritual pride; and pride, we remember, is sometimes said to have been the sin that broke up the
original Eden.

Emerson, of course, was too knowing ever to
have joined himself in the flesh to these altruistic
humbugs; but one cannot forget that he was a
patron of Alcott's and for the most part took that
dilapidated Platonist with portentous seriousness. For instance, he observes in his *Journal* for
1857:

Last night in the conversation Alcott appeared to
great advantage, and I saw again, as often before, his
singular superiority. As pure intellect I have never seen
his equal. The people with whom he talks do not ever
understand him; ... do not know that all they have in
their baby brains is incoherent and spotty; that all he
sees and says is like astronomy, lying there real and
vast, every part and fact in eternal connection with the
whole.

The truth is that Alcott is in a way a caricature of Emerson; but it is just as a caricature that
he shows with startling vividness what Emersonianism runs to when divested of the common
sense and strong character which were ballast to
the master's shining optimism. Emerson saw the
good and radiated spiritual light as few other men
of his century did; but his blindness to the reality
of evil was not of his strength, it was of his weakness. Hence it is that he often loses value for his
admirers in proportion to their maturity and

experience. He is preëminently the poet of religion and philosophy for the young; whereas men as they grow older are inclined to turn from him, in their more serious needs, to those sages who have supplemented insight with a firmer grasp of the whole of human nature.

That is undoubtedly true; nevertheless, as time passes the deficiencies of this brief flowering period of New England, of which Emerson was the perfect spokesman, may well be more and more condoned for its rarity and beauty. One of the wings of the spirit is hope, and nowhere is there to be found a purer hope than in the books of our New England sage; rather, it might be said that he went beyond hope to the assurance of present happiness. The world had never before seen anything quite of this kind, and may not see its like again.

CHARLES ELIOT NORTON

CHARLES ELIOT NORTON

ONE of the mottoes prefixed to the second volume of these letters [1] is a sentence from Sainte-Beuve, which would read in English something like this: "The illustrious writers, the great poets, scarcely exist without having about them other men, themselves essential rather than secondary, great in their incompleteness, the equals in the inner life of thought with those whom they love, whom they serve, and who are kings by right of art." The words could not be more fitting if they had been written with Norton in mind, so perfectly do they express his relation to the artists of his generation. We think of him first, perhaps, as the friend of Ruskin and Carlyle, of Longfellow and Lowell, and of the other writers who were giving lustre to the Victorian and — may we say? — Cantabrigian age, and we recall the epitaph he once playfully suggested for himself: "He had good friends, whom he loved"; but we do his memory wrong if we regard him as a mere parasite or shadow, of those greater reputations. He was more than friend and audience; he was counsellor and, at times, judge. One of the few notes

[1] *Letters of Charles Eliot Norton*. With Biographical Comment, by his daughter Sara Norton and M. A. De Wolfe Howe. Boston: Houghton Mifflin Co., 1913.

of personal resentment in his correspondence is a protest against a passage in Ruskin's *Præterita* which had represented him as seeking unasked the society of the more famous man. Ruskin, indeed, meant to cast no slur, and in the same book adds the most generous praise of his "first tutor":

Norton saw all my weaknesses, measured all my narrownesses, and, from the first, took serenely, and as it seemed of necessity, a kind of paternal authority over me, and a right of guidance — though the younger of the two — and always admitting my full power in its own kind.

Something of that "rectorial power" he had with whomsoever he lived, whether individual or community, and from it came his honour and a measure, too, of bitter reproach. His letters, as they are now published in selection, have other claims to attention, but their greatest value is in the clear revelation of the man himself to those who knew him not at all or, like the writer of this essay, knew him but slightly, and of the source of the authority which made him among his more productive contemporaries an *égal au dedans*. The opportunity to set forth the nature of that power brings a peculiar pleasure, not without a sense also of humility, to the present editor of the journal which Norton helped to found and into which so much of his character entered.[1]

[1] Written in 1913 when I was editing the *Nation*.

As for the work of the editors of these volumes it is sufficient to say that there is not a word of their own about Norton, nor is there a letter of his included, which would have given offence to his scrupulous taste in such matters; and, on the other hand, there is no evidence that anything has been omitted which is necessary to the understanding of the man and his position. Possibly the interest of the volumes would not have been diminished if an even stricter selection had been exercised in the earlier letters. Norton came to maturity rather late, and it is the gravity of his judgment more than any adventitious aids of fancy or cleverness that holds our attention.

His letters in this respect are curiously unlike those of Lowell, with which one naturally compares them. After the first crude effervescence of youth Lowell charms us with his grace and dazzles us with the fecundity of his invention; we say that never was there a fellow like this to amuse and entertain. But somehow the interest does not quite hold to the end; we are a little irked to find that he never entirely controlled his own faculties; we never touch bottom with him, not so much because of the depth of his mind as because of the drift of its currents. With Norton it is just the reverse. We begin by thinking him, comparatively at least, a trifle dull; but as we read on we are caught by the sheer integrity of his language; we are impressed by the feeling that here was a man of utter veracity, who never swerved aside to be funny or wise or profound or original, but was concerned to say with unflinching precision just what he felt and thought. No doubt these virtues have a negative side and denote a certain slowness of imagination and a certain lack of higher spontaneity in the writer, but at the worst we are not annoyed by the attempt to conceal such deficiencies under a sham sprightliness, and at the best we forget them by reason of other positive qualities. There is nothing in this correspondence in any way equivalent to the winged phrases in which Lowell describes to Norton the effect of Emerson's Phi Beta Kappa oration: "It began nowhere and ended everywhere, and yet, as always with that divine man, it left you feeling that something beautiful had passed that way — something more beautiful than anything else, like the rising and setting of stars," etc. Nor was it within the compass of Norton's pen to write any one of a dozen of those improvisations in which Lowell fairly takes your breath away with the audacity of his wit. But neither was it within the scope of Lowell's intelligence to give finality to one of the commonplaces of experience with just such grave and pondered beauty of expression as that which Norton used to Leslie Stephen on the death of his brother: "It is one of those changes which alter the whole habit and aspect of life, — shutting up so many chambers to which nobody else has a key, increasing the solitary and silent part of life which grows so disproportionate to the rest as we grow old." In the end we suspect that most readers will say, as they close the second of these volumes: Here is the larger man and the deeper nature, and here, after all deductions, are the finer letters.

But it must not be supposed that Norton was pedantic or priggish in his correspondence, or sent out an epistle with the solemn consideration of a judge handing down a decision. He is familiar and easy enough on occasion, and at times strong and picturesque. Especially during and after his third long visit abroad his letters and journal gain in substance by the occasional portraits of men and reports of conversations. Naturally, Carlyle is prominent in these, and he is presented as abounding in the kind of humorous exaggeration by virtue of which Norton always defended him against his detractors.[1] One day it is Carlyle discoursing on Browning:

[1] *Haud inexpertus loquor.* There lies before me now a letter from Norton, dated 8 April, 1904, which illustrates this point:

"I am truly obliged to you for sending to me a copy of your interesting paper on *The Spirit of Carlyle*, which I might not have had the pleasure of seeing had it not been for your kindness. . . .

"You will not be surprised at my thinking that you do Froude more than justice, and that in your estimate of his work you hardly recognize how false an impression Froude conveys of the actual life and relations of Carlyle, for it

So he went on till some one asked him if he had seen Browning lately. "Na," said he, with a twinkle in his eye, "but I've read the whole of his new poem, *The Ring and the Book*, in four volumes, from beginning to end, without omitting a word, and a most extraordinary production it is; — a work of great ingenuity and full of verra strikin' sentences. I met Browning, indeed, in Piccadilly the other day, and I told him I'd read his poem from the first word thereof way to the last, and he said to me, quickly, 'Well! Well?' and I replied that I thought it a book of prodigious talent and unparalleled ingenuity; but then, I suppose trusting to the sincerity of my own thoughts, I went on to say that of all the strange books produced on this distracted airth, by any of the sons of Adam, this one was altogether the strangest and the most preposterous in its construction; and where, said I, do ye think to find the eternal harmonies in it? Browning did not seem to be pleased with my speech, and he bade me good morning."

At another time it is Carlyle's swift judgment of Sumner, whom he defines as "the most com-

ought to be held in mind that whatever tendency to mysticism may have controlled Carlyle's conception of life, his actual relations to it were of the simplest character. These actual and natural relations have been distorted by Froude to such a degree that the true impression of the man as he lived is hardly to be obtained from his volumes. The intensity of his domestic affections, the tenderness of his sympathies, his fidelity in the discharge of all duties to his family, were almost as exceptional as his literary genius. He exposed himself to great misapprehensions by his humorous extravagances and by his exaggerated utterances of feeling; but he had one of the simplest and soundest of hearts, and he had a capacity for quick and tender sympathy such as I have known in few other men...."

pletely nothin' of a mon that ever crossed my
threshold, — naught whatsoever in him or of
him but wind and vanity." And again it is Carlyle on Carlyle, expressing a fundamental truth
about himself which some of his critics have still
to learn:

While we were sitting by the fireside, before we left
the house this afternoon, he said, speaking of himself, —
"I've been much misunderstood in my time, and very
lately now I was readin' an article on Froude's view of
Ireland in the last number of *Macmillan*, written by a
man whom ye may have seen, one ——, a willow pat-
tern of a man, very shrill and voluble, but harmless, a
pure herbivorous, nay, graminivorous creature, and he
says with many terms of compliment that there's 'a
great and venerable author' who's done infinite harm to
the world by preachin' the gospel that *Might makes
Right*, which is the verra precise contrary to the truth I
hold and have endeavoured to set forth, which is simply
that *Right makes Might*. And I well remember when, in
my younger days, the force o' this truth first dawned on
me, it was a sort of Theodicee to me, a clew to many
facts to which I have held on from that day."

But it is Norton himself we come to seek in this
correspondence, rather than Carlyle or another,
and Norton's place as the last representative of a
remarkable generation — *ultimus Novorum An-
glicanorum*. Some day we shall appreciate New
England literature at its true value. But before
that day we must learn to distinguish between
what is provincial and what is merely local. If
anything is provincial it is to incorporate such

men as the old Scottish poets in the main body
of English literature, as is commonly done in man-
uals of the subject, and to relegate the Massachusetts writers to an appendix, if they are men-
tioned at all, as though they were foreign to the
spirit of the language in which they wrote. In
one of his letters from London, Lowell tells of a
Scotsman who "had the ill-manners" to compliment him on his English: "Why, I should n't
know you were n't an Englishman. Where did
you get it?" Lowell's was the reproof valiant.
"I could n't resist," he says, "and answered with
a couple of verses from a Scottish ballad —

> I got it in my mither's wame,
> Whaur ye 'll get never the like!

He will never compliment me again, I fear."
Whatever justification there may be for separat-
ing off the New England group would lie rather in
their facile cosmopolitanism. It is true that they
showed symptoms of a weakening at the root
by their too ready submission to influences from
Germany and Spain and Italy, but in the main
they were faithful inheritors of one of the domi-
nant British traditions. Through all the changes
that inevitably came with the passage of two
hundred years, they still remembered the voice
of Bunyan and Baxter and Marvell and Herbert
and Wither and the others to whom their fathers
had hearkened at the time of the great exodus.

They created no one piece quite of the first rank in the realm of the imagination, but the body of their work, when the final account is made, will stand out honourably in the general production of the Victorian era, and the spirit which directed them and which rises from their books as a kind of fine and fragrant exhalation, will be recognized as one of the very precious things in the history of the world.

And Norton himself was fully aware of the beauty and meaning of that tradition into which he was born. No doubt, in the course of his long life he said many hard things about America, speaking sometimes not altogether wisely. Like others of his generation, he was caught up by the enthusiasm of the years when the country was moved to its depths by a passionate idea, and had it not been for ill health he would have fought in the Civil War with the soldiers of his State. But after the war he was never in sympathy with certain marked tendencies of democracy and never hesitated to express his opinion. "I have been too much of an idealist about America," he wrote, near the end of his life, "had set my hopes too high, had formed too fair an image of what she might become. Never had nation such an opportunity, she was the hope of the world." This disillusion was in part due to his fastidious social sense, sharpened by the contrast of America with the large opportunities he had enjoyed. Society was to him "the very rarest and best thing that the world proper can give us. It is the thing that our modern materialism is largely killing out, — that is, in its highest form, the society that bears witness to leisure and culture, and good breeding, made up of men who, though versed in affairs, are still idealists and lovers of poetry." This was the idea he had in mind, no doubt, when he began a lecture on the word "gentleman" before a large class with the grave pleasantry: "None of you, probably, has ever seen a gentleman." Such sentiments and words were not always taken kindly, and when, as at the time of the Spanish War, he did not hesitate to expose publicly the mixture of hypocrisy and thoughtlessness that entered into the popular furor, resentment against him became almost a mark of loyalty to the country. Opinions may vary in regard to his tilt with Senator Hoar; there are those who still think he was rightly rebuked for "the habit of bitter and sneering speech"; but these, we may believe, are not many. Reading the letters of Norton and Senator Hoar side by side, most of us to-day will feel that honour and truth are rather on the side of Norton, and his address to the Cambridge Club, which, in a garbled report, called forth the storm of reproach, will seem the memorable utterance of a calm and virile patriotism. Nor should it be forgotten that the address ended

with the strong words, "*Nil desperandum de re-
publica.*" Norton himself did, in fact, never despair. Many times in his letters he expresses his
faith in the essential soundness of the people. It
is notable that the architecture of the World's
Fair at Chicago was to him a magnificent achievement and a greater promise, and that from the
city itself he could draw happy auguries for the
future of America. A Brahmin of New England
who can admire Chicago is not quite lost to virtue.

But withal, whether for his credit or discredit,
it must be admitted that Norton stood before the
country and exercised the office of critic as the
product of a particular time and place. He was
of Cambridge, the earlier Cambridge which was,
with Concord, one of the eyes of New England,
the Greece of Greece, so to speak; and this position he never forgot. Several times in his letters
he refers to the exceptional character of the generation in which his own life began. "I believe,
indeed," he says once, writing at the end of the
century, "that the very pleasantest little oasis of
space and time was that of New England from
about the beginning of the century to about 1825
[he himself was born in 1827]. The spirit of that
time was embodied in Emerson, in Longfellow,
in Holmes, and in Lowell. It was an inexperi-
enced and youthful spirit, but it was a happy one;
it had the charm of youth, its hope, its simplicity,

its sweetness." He might have added, as his
reader no doubt added, that he, too, was one of
the bearers of that spirit — *sacra fero ingenti per-
cussus amore* — though, for the hopefulness of
youth, he brought other qualities. Innumerable
forces of inheritance made him what he was. His
ancestor, John Norton, named for his more noted
uncle, one of the four famous Johns (Cotton,
Norton, Wilson, and Davenport), took charge of
the parish of Hingham in 1678. In the same year
he published a poem, being nothing other than a
*Funeral Elegy, Upon that Patron of Virtue, the
truly pious, peerless & matchless Gentlewoman,
Mrs. Anne Bradstreet.* In 1897 our Norton edited
the poems of the matchless gentlewoman, and in
his introduction wrote of her with more than his
usual freedom and intimacy:

It struck me that there would be something of quaint
appropriateness in my writing, at this long interval, in
regard to her whose praises he [John Norton] had sung,
and that the act would not be without a certain piety
toward my ancestor. And, further, I reflected, that as I
could trace my descent in one line directly from Governor Thomas Dudley, the father of Mrs. Bradstreet,
and as portraits of her brother, Governor Joseph Dudley, and his wife, looked down on me every day while I
sat at breakfast and dinner, she, as my Aunt many
times removed, might not unjustly have a claim upon
me for such token of respect to her memory as had been
asked of me. . . . She cherished in herself and in her children the things of the mind and of the spirit; and if such
memory as her verses have secured for her depend rather

on the circumstance of a woman's writing them at the time when she did, and in the place where she lived, than upon their poetic worth, it is a memory honourable to her, and it happily preserves the name of a good woman, among whose descendants has been more than one poet whose verses reflect lustre on her own. (Through one of her children she is the ancestress of Richard Henry Dana; through another, of Oliver Wendell Holmes.)

From a daughter of John Norton, married to John Quincy, was descended John Quincy Adams. In the direct male line came Andrews Norton, who in 1811 was appointed a tutor at Harvard and later professor of sacred literature. In 1821 he married Catharine Eliot (whence the relationship with President Eliot), and soon bought the house with some fifty acres of land in Cambridge known as Shady Hill. In that quiet home, which was to welcome so many of the great scholars and writers of the world, and whose gracious courtesies and dignity so many Harvard men still cherish in memory as a possession equal in value to any learning, Charles Eliot Norton, one of four children who grew to maturity, was born, and there, after many years and many labours, laid down his life.

By every right of tradition Norton belonged with the group of scholars and poets who just preceded him in birth, and he belonged with them also by virtue of his own accomplishments. When we consider the work of that generation it seems as if we saw the energy of a strong people, nourished through long discipline and austere abstentions, now suddenly freed from repression and displaying itself in manifold, and all too brief, expansion. Each man had his particular share in that activity: to one it was the exercise of wit, to another the sentiment of home and hearth, to another the comfort of religion, to another the re-creation of aboriginal life, to another the critical judgment, to another the symbolism of a brooding imagination, to another the freedom of nature, to another the justification of the untrammelled spirit. Now it must be admitted that in none of these fields was Norton quite pre-eminent; even as a critic his writing falls below Whipple's, who was nevertheless in every way a smaller man than he. It is not unlikely that the melancholy which shows itself occasionally in his letters was in some small measure due to the consciousness of these deficiencies. So he writes one day to Lowell: "Except for George [William Curtis], I have been very solitary. From year to year I seem to myself to grow more and more silent, and to express less of what is in my soul. I should like to have the power of expression, — at least long enough to give form and utterance to a few of the deepest conceptions of Life and its significance and uses which come to one as one grows old and draws the lessons from his own experience." It is true, as he says, that he never embodied his wisdom of experience in literary form, but this wisdom is precisely what he stood for among his contemporaries, and just because we feel this in his letters we shall treasure them. He was, in the best sense of the word, the man of culture, the ripe scholar, to whom the lessons of the past had become a personal experience. To the multiform flowering of the time he brought the note of sound cosmopolitanism.

But he brought also with that culture, and this was his largest gift, a peculiar virtue of inheritance. More than any other man of his group, he represented the naked New England conscience and its tenacity of character. It may seem that his powers were manifested chiefly in negation. To the individual, and particularly to the young student who showed promise of achievement, he could be generous of help and encouragement. But in relation to the community at large he stood undeniably as critic and check; and this attitude was often deeply resented. What has this man done, people would ask in a tone of cavilling rebellion, that he should set himself up as judge over others? Well, the question was not unnatural; yet is not character always in some way negative? Is it not of its very essence to act as a check upon the impulsive temperament, and even upon the ranging enthusiasms of the soul? And especially in the hour of expansive liberty that came to New England when it had broken from the bondage of religion, it was desirable that the principle of restraint, broadened indeed by contact with the world, but not weakened or clouded, should have had its voice and embodiment. On the ship which brought Norton home from Europe in May of 1873 Emerson also sailed, and we have in Norton's journal a record of his wonderful conversation, with the journalist's comment and criticism. For one who reflects on the later course of New England and America these are memorable pages:

Emerson was the greatest talker in the ship's company. He talked with all men, and yet was fresh and zealous for talk at night. His serene sweetness, the pure whiteness of his soul, the reflection of his soul in his face, were never more apparent to me; but never before in intercourse with him had I been so impressed with the limits of his mind. His optimistic philosophy has hardened into a creed, with the usual effects of a creed in closing the avenues of truth.... He refuses to believe in disorder or evil. Order is the absolute law; disorder is but a phenomenon....

But such inveterate and persistent optimism, though it may show only its pleasant side in such a character as Emerson's, is dangerous doctrine for a people. It degenerates into fatalistic indifference to moral considerations, and to personal responsibilities; it is at the root of much of the irrational sentimentalism in our American politics....

Never were truer words put on paper. The pure whiteness of Emerson's soul is, when all has been reckoned up, the finest thing that New England has given to the world; but in the society for which he ministered as a high priest of ecstatic vision, there was a place also, an indispensable place, for the questioner who stood for the traditional New England conscience and sense of evil. We shall do well to honour Norton in our memory as one who through all spiritual temptations kept his feet firmly planted on the bedrock of character.

The winds of folly blew about him as they blow about us, the dust of pedantries smote his eyes, cant and sentimentalism fouled his air, but he held to his course unmoved, cherishing always in his heart what is lovely and of good report, a faithful teacher, to whom were well applied the words of the poet who had been the chief study of his life:

Felice te, che sì parli a tua posta.

HENRY ADAMS

HENRY ADAMS

THE display of a copy of *The Education of Henry Adams* has been a kind of hall-mark of distinction for any private library, ever since the book was printed and distributed to a few friends of the author in 1907. Even to have read its jealously guarded pages was something to boast of, and the initiated were wont to wag their heads over its revelations as over some exotic drink which they were expected to admire, but which teased their palate by its strange flavour. And now the volume is published to the world, and one wonders what the world will make of it — perhaps nothing. Yet simply as the record of an unusual life it is certainly entertaining above the average, and would be doubly so were it half as long. The virtue of cynicism is its point, and only the genial can afford to be diffuse. Mr. Adams was nothing if not cynical; had he learned the rare art of compression, he might have produced a work worthy of a place beside the autobiographies of Gibbon and Franklin.

No other man of this country, save his brothers, one of whom, the late Charles Francis Adams, has followed his example, had quite such material at his disposal. Son of the elder Charles Francis Adams, grandson of a President, and great-grandson of the mighty John of Revolutionary fame, his conscience was a kind of historical epitome. As private secretary of his father at the British court during the Civil War, he saw the inside of that society and government towards whose public manifestation his family had lived in a state of hereditary feud. As a member of the Harvard faculty for seven years, he is said to have introduced the first historical seminary into an American college. As an author, not to mention his privately printed *Mont-Saint-Michel and Chartres* (recently republished by the authority of the American Institute of Architects) and his unacknowledged novels *Esther* and *Democracy*, he produced a history of the United States under Jefferson and Madison notable for its original and broad use of sources, for its judicious characterizations, and its sustained interest. As a citizen of Washington, where his later and some of his earlier years were spent, he saw familiarly the working of a government which he admired no more than he did that of London. As a friend, he was close to John Hay and Clarence King, great men in this field, the latter especially, though little known to the world, yet by the few idolized as the *deus præsens* of social joy and wisdom.

Not many men of the past generation enjoyed such opportunities of watching the drama of life, and perhaps none of them excelled him in the

power of penetrating beneath the surface of
things; and this power is none the less amazing
when, as often happened with him, the lifted cur-
tain, behind which we looked for the revelation
of some well-staged scene of history, exhibited
only the disarray of planless confusion. That
indeed is the moral of the book — if moral it may
be called — the baffled sense of mystery behind
the veil of apparent design. "King and Hay and
Adams could neither of them escape floundering
through the corridors of chaos," he says, with
an ungrammatical reminiscence of Longfellow,
"that opened as they passed to the end."

But this is to anticipate. What we have to note
now is the pungent interest of Adams's comments
on the figures thrown up in flashes of light beside
him as he journeyed through these shadowy corridors. Sometimes it is a whole society that furnished him with a discharge of epigrams. First
it is the people among whom he was born, and
who stamped their traits upon his own soul:

Resistance to something was the law of New England
nature; the boy looked out on the world with the instinct of resistance; for numberless generations his
predecessors had viewed the world chiefly as a thing to
be reformed, filled with evil forces to be abolished, and
they saw no reason to suppose that they had wholly
succeeded in the abolition; the duty was unchanged.
That duty implied not only resistance to evil, but hatred
of it. Boys naturally look on all force as an enemy, and
generally find it so, but the New Englander, whether

boy or man, in his long struggle with a stingy or hostile universe, had learned also to love the pleasure of hating; his joys were few.

Beside this one might set his summary characterization of the opposite type as he came into contact with it as a Harvard undergraduate: "Strictly, the southerner had no mind; he had temperament. He was not a scholar; he had no intellectual training; he could not analyse an idea, and he could not even conceive of admitting two; but in life one could get along very well without ideas, if one had only the social instinct." To complete the gallery I may quote his report of a national trait which had exercised the wit of Shakespeare and Swift and Horace Walpole and a long succession of observers of human nature as minted in Great Britain.

The English themselves [he remarks while in London] hardly conceived that their mind was either economical, sharp, or direct; but the defect that most struck an American was its enormous waste in eccentricity. Americans needed and used their whole energy, and applied it with close economy; but English society was eccentric by law and for sake of the eccentricity itself. The commonest phrase overheard at an English club or dinner-table was that so-and-so "is quite mad." It was no offense to so-and-so; it hardly distinguished him from his fellows; and when applied to a public man, like Gladstone, it was qualified by epithets much more forcible. Eccentricity was so general as to become hereditary distinction. It made the chief charm of English society as well as its chief terror.

The epigrammatic flavour is sufficient to lend
some freshness to a truism as old as Hamlet's
clown, but Adams's further query whether this
eccentricity is a sign of strength or weakness, and
his remarks on its working when brought into
conflict with the plainer methods of his father
and Thurlow and William Evarts, add a quality
of reflection that is not at all trite. Nor did his
keen understanding forsake him when dealing
with individuals, as might be instanced by his
characterizations of the men just named, or of
such other politicians as Grant and McKinley
and their Cabinets. Of mere anecdote the pages
contain comparatively little, although here and
there a good story gets entangled in his web of
comment. Those who have some knowledge of
Henry Reeve, the solemn, bulky, busy, doc-
trinaire editor of the *Edinburgh Review*, and of
the Grotes, will be amused by this rencontre.
"Every one," says Adams, "had heard of Mrs.
Grote as 'the origin of the word grotesque.'
Every one had laughed at the story of Reeve approaching Mrs. Grote, with his usual somewhat
florid manner, asking in his literary dialect how
her husband the historian was: — 'And how is
the learned Grotius?' 'Pretty well, thank you,
Puffendorf!' One winced at the word, as though
it were a drawing of Forain." Best of all, best of
all at least for the lover of literature who tempers
his enthusiasms with a grain of hard-headed cyni-

cism, is Adams's account of meeting with Swinburne at the home of Lord Houghton, and this pendant to it of a later date:

Ten years afterwards Adams met him [Swinburne] at the Geneva Conference, fresh from Paris, bubbling with delight at a call he had made on Hugo: — "I was shown into a large room," he said, "with women and men seated in chairs against the walls, and Hugo at one end throned. No one spoke. At last Hugo raised his voice solemnly, and uttered the words: — 'Quant à moi, je crois en Dieu!' Silence followed. Then a woman responded as if in deep meditation: — 'Chose sublime! un Dieu qui croit en Dieu!'"

But it is not as a gallery of character etchings or as a repertory of stories that Mr. Adams's book mainly interests us; it is always the observer more than the observed that holds our attention, the effect being much the same as if we were reading a novel of Henry James, in which we are less concerned with the narrated acts of a group of men and women than with the colour these actions will take in the mind of some outside spectator, revealed or half-revealed. With both the novelist and the biographer the impelling motive is curiosity rather than sympathy; but with a difference. In James we feel more the detachment of a mere psychological experimenter, the unconcern of one who creates a world of complex emotions and wills for the somewhat chilly pleasure of taking apart what he has so carefully put together; whereas in Adams there is always present the eager desire to discover in the drama some elusive truth which, if found, would give a meaning to its unfolding scenes. The autobiography is well named *The Education of Henry Adams*, though we surmise from the beginning that no lesson will ever be learned, and that the learner has set himself to decipher a text in a foreign tongue without grammar or lexicon in his hands.

In a way the text before him was not one of his own choice, but forced on him by birth and inheritance. This breed of New England, of whom he was so consciously a titled representative, had once come out from the world for the sake of a religious and political affirmation — the two were originally one — to confirm which they were ready to deny all the other values of life. For the liberty to follow this affirmation they would discard tradition and authority and form and symbol and all that ordinarily binds men together in the bonds of habit. But the liberty of denying may itself become a habit. The intellectual history of New England is in fact the record of the encroachment of this liberty on the very affirmation for which it was at first the bulwark. By a gradual elimination of its positive content the faith of the people had passed from Calvinism to Unitarianism, and from this to free thinking, until in the days of our Adams there was little left to the intellect but a great denial:

Of all the conditions of his youth which afterwards puzzled the grown up man, this disappearance of religion puzzled him most. The boy went to church twice every Sunday; he was taught to read his Bible, and he learned religious poetry by heart; he believed in a mild Deism; he prayed; he went through all the forms; but neither to him nor to his brothers or sisters was religion real. Even the mild discipline of the Unitarian church was so irksome that they all threw it off at the first possible moment, and never afterwards entered a church. The religious instinct had vanished, and could not be revived, although one made in later life many efforts to recover it. That the most powerful emotion of man, next to the sexual, should disappear, might be a personal defect of his own; but that the most intelligent society, led by the most intelligent clergy, in the most moral conditions he ever knew, should have solved all the problems of the universe so thoroughly as to have quite ceased making itself anxious about past or future, and should have persuaded itself that all the problems which had convulsed human thought from earliest recorded time, were not worth discussing, seemed to him the most curious social phenomenon he had to account for in a long life.

So the original affirmation had been swallowed up in its own defences, while the negative impulse grew "to a degree that in the long run became positive and hostile." But with this intellectual negation there remained almost in full force the moral impulse which from the first had been so intimately associated with a negative separatism. This is the key we must hold in our hands if we would enter into the inner life of Henry Adams and the other New Englanders of his generation, taking the word broadly — we must, if possible, put ourselves into the state of men whose conscience was moving, so to speak, *in vacuo*, like a dispossessed ghost seeking a substantial habitation. Adams "tended towards negation on his own account, as one side of the New England mind had always done." In this vacuum various minds sought relief in various ways, connecting themselves naturally with the contemporary currents of European thought. Emerson, as the purest spirit of them all, would rest in the bare liberty of prophesying, in the security of an intuition content in itself and careless of all preceding experience as formulated in law and custom. He was *par excellence* the pure Romantic, yet withal a New Englander at heart, not a German. John Fiske, if we may extend the limits of a generation so far, looked to the new discoveries of scientific evolution to give substance to the vague cosmic deity which had swum into the place of the Christian Jehovah. Most significant of all in some respects for our present subject is the case of Charles Eliot Norton. With him New England scepticism merges into the contented agnosticism of his British friends, particularly of Leslie Stephen, while the sting of conscience takes the form of distress at the licence of an agnostic society. So he writes, in one vein to Goldwin Smith:

Possibly I regret less than you do the giving up of the

old faith, and the being compelled to renounce as hopeless every attempt to solve the problems which excite our curiosity. The position toward the universe in which we find ourselves seems to me on the whole the manliest which has been attained. We are thrown back on our own resources to make the best of our lives. A new sense of responsibility is aroused in us, and, by the narrowing of the limits of our hopes and expectations, we find ourselves more capable of using our faculties for legitimate and rational ends.

But when the conscience of Norton is speaking we hear words very different from those of his reason just quoted. So, for instance, he writes to Leslie Stephen:

It looks as if the world were entering on a new stage of experience, unlike anything heretofore, in which there must be a new discipline of suffering to fit men for the new conditions. I fear that America is beginning a long course of error and of wrong, and is likely to become more and more a power for disturbance and for barbarism. The worst sign is the lack of seriousness in the body of the people; its triviality, and its indifference to moral principle.

Norton was not consistent, you will say; and rightly. There is a question to ask of a man who finds a new source of responsibility in a creed destructive of the very principle of authority, yet laments the lack of responsibility in a world that acts in accordance with such a creed; there is a beautiful inconsistency in the heart of one who professes complete agnosticism, yet spends his life in the devoted study of Dante. It is the inconsistency of a conscience that has outlived faith and not found philosophy, the will of New England working out in its own peculiar manner the problem of the nineteenth century. To Adams the question of meaning in the world came with a somewhat different emphasis. Norton was the product of a long line of theologians, and doubt, when it crept in, took primarily the form of philosophical scepticism. But Adams was not born into the Brahmin caste. From the beginning, as seen in his great-grandfather and in his ancestral cousin, the revolt against traditional authority had been rather in the field of politics, and it was in his blood, so to speak, that his agnosticism should strike first upon the belief in a providential purpose in history. That indeed is the stimulus of what he calls his education. His inquiry was to branch out into a wider sphere, and in the end was to make its return to a medieval mysticism, as Norton's did to a medieval æstheticism; but in his earlier years he was sufficiently absorbed in seeking some theory to explain the sequence of historical events. What was the meaning of this opposition which his forbears and his father had maintained against the settled institutions of government? To whose profit did it accrue, or was there any profit to be found anywhere? In what way had the world grown wiser and truer from this struggle and from all the struggles of men since the beginning of time?

Where should he put his finger on the thread of progress in the terrible tangle of human misadventure?

He began his inquiry — at least in old age, looking back over his experience, he seemed to himself to have begun it — when as a boy he watched the political manœuvres of the Abolitionists. At home he "lived in the atmosphere of the Stamp Act, the Tea Tax, and the Boston Massacre"; only now "the Slave Power took the place of Stuart Kings and Roman Popes." He observed his father and Charles Sumner and their clique play the game of politics against the entrenched aristocracy of Boston; he saw from the inside the working of the coalition which sent Sumner to the Senate and made George Boutwell the Democratic governor of Massachusetts; he thought their ends noble, such as his great-grandfather would have approved, but he knew that their means were ignoble; and he wondered. "Thus before he was fifteen years old, he had managed to get himself into a state of moral confusion from which he never escaped."

Formal instruction gave him no clue to the labyrinth. "Four years of Harvard College, if successful, resulted in an autobiographical blank, a mind on which only a water-mark had been stamped." He got no wisdom from his teachers, none from his fellow students, though these included such promising names as Alexander Agassiz, Phillips Brooks, H. H. Richardson, and O. W. Holmes. "The chief wonder of education," he remarks, "is that it does not ruin everybody connected with it, teachers and taught." That is the world-old ingratitude of the scholar, commonly pronounced most vigorously by those who have profited most from instruction; it falls naturally from the lips of Henry Adams, and perhaps with him means something. At any rate he left college still "watching vaguely for a path and a direction." Travel might bestow what the class-room had withheld. He travelled. In Rome, more than once, he sat at sunset on the steps of the church of Santa Maria di Ara Cœli — there where Gibbon had mused on the fall of empire — sat, and reflected, and concluded nothing:

Rome was a bewildering complex of ideas, experiments, ambitions, energies; without her, the Western world was pointless and fragmentary; she gave heart and unity to it all; yet Gibbon might have gone on for the whole century, sitting among the ruins of the Capitol, and no one would have passed, capable of telling him what it meant. Perhaps it meant nothing.

We need not follow Adams through all the stages of his historical education. One great lesson in negative wisdom he was to learn in London, while helping his father to unravel the machinations of Palmerston and Lord John Russell and Gladstone against the government of the United States. He was to observe men sensitive

to any imputation of untruth and otherwise
highly moral, yet in public speaking one thing
while in private acting another, men whose courage, as it seemed to him, lay in subterfuge and
whose honour went no further than indignation.
"If one could not believe them, Truth in politics
might be ignored as a delusion"; and he had ample
grounds for not believing any word of Gladstone
at least, the most righteous of them all. What was
to be made out of such a contradiction in terms
by a student of life who "liked lofty moral
principles and cared little for political tactics"?
"Here, then, appeared in its fullest force, the practical difficulty in education which a mere student
could never overcome; a difficulty not in theory,
or knowledge, or even want of experience, but in
the sheer chaos of human nature."

That difficulty was not diminished when he
returned to Washington and saw a blunt plain
soldier like Grant entangled in the most question-
able business. For one moment, indeed, at the
time of our Spanish War, he felt a sense of possible purpose working itself out in history. To
him, if to no one else, "still living in the atmosphere of Palmerston and John Russell, the sudden appearance of Germany as the grizzly terror
which, in twenty years, effected what Adamses
had tried for two hundred in vain,—frightened
England into America's arms,—seemed as melo-
dramatic as any plot of Napoleon the Great." But

his satisfaction was more temperamental than intellectual—than intelligent, one might say—and in the embroglio of foreign intrigue that followed, and that wrecked the health of his dearest friend, John Hay, he was forced to see again only the conflict of blind wills and the shifting combinations of chance.

If Adams's observation of history in the making, supplemented by his study of history in the past, led to these sceptical conclusions, a sudden event of a more personal sort seemed, as it were, to rend the veil of cosmic charity and to show him that the foolishness of human affairs was but a little centre of chaos encompassed by a vast and malignant chaos of nature. Called from London to Italy by a telegram, he found his beloved sister, a woman of forty, for whom life had been gay and brilliant, dying in extreme torture from a miserable accident. As he sat by her bedside and watched the agony of her dissolution, while out of doors the world was glowing with the sensuous joys of an Italian summer, it seemed to him that now for the first time he beheld Nature face to face; and what he saw in that vision was to haunt him for the rest of his years:

Impressions like these are not reasoned or catalogued in the mind; they are felt as part of violent emotion; and the mind that feels them is a different one from that which reasons; it is thought of a different power and a different person. The first serious consciousness of Nature's gesture — her attitude towards life — took form then as a fantasm, a nightmare, an insanity of force. For the first time, the stage-scenery of the senses collapsed; the human mind felt itself stripped naked, vibrating in a void of shapeless energies, with resistless mass, colliding, crushing, wasting and destroying what these same energies had created and laboured from eternity to perfect. Society became fantastic, a vision of pantomime with a mechanical motion; and its so-called thought merged in the mere sense of life, and pleasure in the sense. The usual anodynes of social medicine became evident artifice. Stoicism was perhaps the best; religion was the most human; but the idea that any personal deity could find pleasure or profit in torturing a poor woman, by accident, with a fiendish cruelty known to man only in perverted and insane temperaments, could not be held for a moment. For pure blasphemy, it made pure atheism a comfort. God might be, as the Church said, a Substance, but he could not be a Person.

In those hours of biting agony, while the individual life so dear to him was wrestling unequally with the unsympathetic powers of death, Adams saw the destiny of mankind merged into the destiny of the sum of things. At an early period he had added to his reading of history a faithful study of science, and as he had sought for a thread of providential guidance in the one, so, under the influence of the newly based theory of evolution, he looked for signs of design and progress in the non-human order of creation. At first the two fields of inquiry had lain apart, but now, as I say, they appeared as phases only of the one problem which engaged his passionate attention. But the search baffled him, baffled him the more as it became more complex. As in history he thought he saw the evil persisting unchanged along with the good, so in the field of science he beheld the lower order of existence continuing on with the higher and throwing an element of stable confusion into progressive mutation. More than that. When he went beyond the material of biology into the dark background of inorganic forces he learned that the physicists themselves acknowledged only an inexpressible mystery. In Germany he heard Haeckel avowing that "the proper essence of substance appeared to him more and more marvellous and enigmatic as he penetrated further into the knowledge of its attributes, — matter and energy, — and as he learned to know their innumerable phenomena and their evolution." In France he heard the clearer and more authoritative voice of Poincaré making the same confession of ignorance: "[in science] we are led to act as though a simple law, when other things were equal, must be more probable than a complicated law. Half a century ago one frankly confessed it, and proclaimed that nature loves simplicity. She has since given us too often the lie. To-day this tendency is no longer avowed, and only so much of it is preserved as is indispensable so that science shall not become impossible." Then, turning to England, he read such words as these: "In the chaos behind sensation, in the 'beyond' of sense-impressions, we cannot infer necessity, order, or routine, for these are concepts formed by the mind of man on this side of sense-impressions. . . . Briefly, chaos is all that science can logically assert of the super-sensuous." Thus as the "unknowable" came nearer to man's inquiry it seemed to put on positive and menacing hues; the pronouncements of the most advanced physical thinkers echoed to Adams what he had learnt from his own study in history — chaos in the background here and there. And if he went to the pseudo-science of psychology he was faced with another "sub-conscious chaos below the mind"; man's "normal thought," he learned, "was dispersion, sleep, dream, inconsequence; the simultaneous action of different thought-centres without central control. His artificial balance was acquired habit. He was an acrobat, with a dwarf on his back, crossing a chasm on a slack-rope, and commonly breaking his neck." Here was a question that sprang from something very far from idle curiosity. Had Adams not witnessed the terror of the mystery, when this thing called chaos had suddenly lurched forward out of its background of mystery and enveloped his little oasis of well-loved order?

What was the proper attitude towards this enigma? Was it that no one can reach beyond himself? "All that Henry Adams ever saw in man was a reflection of his own ignorance" —

such was his political discernment far back in his London days; should that be the final verdict of all his seeing? In a way he had acquired what ages ago had been proclaimed by Socrates as the beginning of wisdom: not to think we know what we do not know. Into this sea of negation he had sailed from the ancient moorings of his people; but not even the New Englander of the nineteenth century could rest in pure negation. Emerson, like Socrates, had found no difficulty in combining scepticism with an intuition of pure spirituality, though, unlike Socrates, to maintain his inner vision intact he shut his eyes resolutely on the darker facts of nature. That serene indifference to evil was the last thing possible to Adams. Another New Englander, nearer to Adams in date, John Fiske, had accepted the most rigid deductions of biological evolution, and then on Darwin's law of natural selection, which for humanly felt good and evil substituted a conception of blind unfeeling mechanism, had superimposed the conception of a cosmic deity unfolding the world to

> one far-off divine event,
> To which the whole creation moves.

Whatever may be said of such a philosophy, it was meaningless to Henry Adams; he could not marry the faith in a benignant pantheistic will with the sort of chaos that lurked for him behind every door of our ignorance. Still another New

Englander, Charles Eliot Norton, as we have
seen, was content to profess a complete agnosticism of theory along with an unswerving belief
in human responsibility — to what? Alas, that
"what" was the little irksome word that Adams
could not get out of his mind.

The answer, or the direction towards an answer, came to him as he walked the halls of the
Paris Exposition of 1900. There, at least, under
the guidance of his scientific friend, Langley, if
he saw nothing that pointed to a rational design
at the end of things, he beheld in the great gallery
of machines a symbol of what science had substituted for design. "The planet itself seemed less
impressive, in its old-fashioned, deliberate, an-
nual or daily revolution, than this huge wheel,
revolving within arm's-length at some vertiginous
speed, and barely murmuring, — scarcely hum-
ming an audible warning to stand a hair's-
breadth further for respect of power, — while it
would not wake the baby lying close against its
frame. Before the end, one began to pray to it;
inherited instinct taught the natural expression
of man before silent and infinite force. Among
the thousand symbols of ultimate energy, the
dynamo was not so human as some, but it was
the most expressive." Force, he would say, blind
whirling force, strapped and bound in iron, is
supreme over all:

> Dinos has driven out Zeus and rules as king.

We should need, in fact, a living Aristophanes to
celebrate this step of a New Englander's education. Other men of the century had discovered
this same god, but their worship had taken
strangely different forms. "Power is power,"
says Tolstoy, reading for himself the lesson of
history at the conclusion of his *War and Peace*,
"that is Power is a word, the true meaning of
which is to us incomprehensible"; and then, as a
good humanitarian, he personifies this Unknowable in the instinctive soul of the People. Nietzsche, too, had found only *Macht* at the heart of
the world, but he worshipped this Power not at
all in the impulse of the People — quite the contrary; and some of his interpreters have deified
a *Schrecklichkeit* very different from the pity of
Tolstoy. Perhaps the true lesson of our age
would be to learn why and how this modern
Janus of Power has tricked us into believing that
he has only one face. But Adams was too knowing to bow the knee with Tolstoy, and too timid
to salute with Nietzsche. He took another way.

Norton, as we have seen, had found agnosticism compatible with devotion to Dante, being
able at least to sympathize with the energetic
moral sense and the æsthetic vision of that poet;
and Adams, like him, turned at last for consolation to the age of Dante, if not to Dante himself,
though with a difference. From the Exposition,
"caring but little for the name, and fixed only on

tracing Force, Adams had gone straight to the
Virgin at Chartres, and asked her to show him
God, face to face, as she did for St. Bernard."
What the Virgin revealed to him is told clearly
enough in the autobiography, but for its fullest
elucidation one should read that extraordinary
disquisition on the art and poetry and philosophy
and religion of the twelfth and thirteenth centuries which he entitles *Mont-Saint-Michel and
Chartres*. In the Virgin Mother of God, to whose
honour the cathedrals pointed their arches
towards heaven, before whose throne the windows were made to glow like the jewels of a
queen, for whose delight romance wove its shim-
mering web of words, to whom great scholars
sacrificed their learning, our far-travelled New
Englander saw at last the one symbol of Force
comprehensible to the human heart, if not to the
human brain. "The Puritans," he says, "aban-
doned the New Testament and the Virgin in
order to go back to the beginning, and renew the
quarrel with Eve"; our latest Puritan rediscov-
ers woman on her medieval throne, and chants to
her in modern speech the ancient pæan to Alma
Venus Genetrix. It would be a pretty business to
unravel the various motives that had impelled
him on this devious way from the sturdy, if un-
loving, protestantism of his race. He himself
makes much of the motive of love as the aspect
of infinite power which man can understand.

That may be; but I suspect that another attribute of the Virgin meant even more to his mind. Read, if you will, his charming pages on her interventions and miracles; you will observe that they were almost without exception performed to override the course of law and justice, and you will learn that behind her woman's pity there was another quality which Adams, at any rate, does not hesitate to glorify as equally feminine:

The fact, conspicuous above all other historical certainties about religion, that the Virgin was by essence illogical, unreasonable, and feminine, is the only fact of any ultimate value worth studying, and starts a number of questions that history has shown itself clearly afraid to touch.... She was imposed unanimously by all classes, because what man wanted most in the Middle Ages was not merely law or equity, but also and particularly favour.... The individual rebelled against restraint; society wanted to do what it pleased; all disliked the laws which Church and State were trying to fasten on them. ... If the Trinity was in its essence Unity, the Mother alone could represent whatever was not Unity; whatever was irregular, exceptional, outlawed; and this was the whole human race.

Conscience was the last tie of New England to its past. Was it the perfect irresponsibility of the Virgin, human no doubt, feminine perhaps, certainly not Puritan, that gave to our tired sceptic the illusion of having reached a comfortable goal after his long voyage of education? There is a fateful analogy between the irresponsibility of unreasoning Force and unreasoning love; and the gods of Nietzsche and of Tolstoy are but the two faces of one god. To change the metaphor, if it may be done without disrespect, the image in the cathedral of Chartres looks perilously like the ancient idol of Dinos decked out in petticoats.

If we regard Adams's scholarship, his imagination, his verbal dexterity, his candour, his cynical vivacity, his range of reflection, we must give him a high place in the American literature of the past generation, a higher place probably than his present limited popularity would indicate. But one winces a little at acknowledging that the latest spokesman of the Adamses and of New England ends his career in sentimental nihilism. From Harvard College, which to Adams had been only one stage in the way of disillusion, the boy John Fiske had written: "When we come to a true philosophy, and make *that* our stand-point, all things become clear. We know what things to learn, and what, in the infinite mass of things, to leave unlearned; and then the Universe becomes clear and harmonious." The tragedy of Adams's education is that of a man who could not rest easy in negation, yet could find no positive faith to take its place. From one point of view he may appear to be the most honest and typical mind of New England in its last condition; yet withal some manlier voice, some word of deeper insight that yet faces the facts of life, we must still expect to hear from the people of Mather and Edwards and Channing and Emerson.

EVOLUTION AND THE OTHER WORLD

EVOLUTION AND THE OTHER WORLD

WHAT special students of so-called psychic phenomena will think of Mr. Henry Holt's two generous volumes [1] I do not know, but to me, and no
doubt to many like me, they are quite the most
important and significant, as they are the most
entertaining, exposition of the subject. This is
indeed something more than a dead book; it is a
life — as it were the voice of a friend confiding
to us through the hours of a long winter night the
lessons, still mingled with hesitations and questions, of his ripe experience. The publicity of
high spirits may abound; but there are pages
also which will reveal their full meaning only to
those who know the author as a friend in the lit-
eral sense of the word, passages, for those who
understand, of almost sacred privacy. So, for
instance, the minute account of the spectacle unfolding at sunrise to the eyes of the watcher at
the author's summer home has its place and
weight for all readers as an argument that, as
these lovely things are far beyond "our ancestors'
universe of darkness and silence," so there may be
infinite ranges of perception still to be discovered

---

[1] *On the Cosmic Relations.* By Henry Holt. Boston:
Houghton Mifflin Co., 1914; second edition, 1919, title
changed to *The Cosmic Relations and Immortality.*

by mankind; but to one who has entered that hospitable "gate, open to all who care to come," and with the kindly guidance of his host has seen the sunlight falling from mountain top to valley and from valley to lake, the printed words will be something more than the speech of a book to its unseen audience. These matters I should like to dwell on for their pleasantness and their wisdom; but, like a bad talker, I must use all my time in contradiction. For I need not defer saying that Mr. Holt's work seems to me to consist of two elements strangely compounded. Besides the appealing sagacity of the man of the world, inquisitive, sceptical of dogma, tolerant of all things except impertinence, resting finally in balance and measure — besides this sagacity of experience to which I bow, there is also in the book a philosophy of a more formal sort, to which, from the deepest knowledge of my heart, I am bound to demur.

Mr. Holt is avowedly of the school of "Lyell, Darwin, Spencer, Huxley, and their friends," who swept away "the flood of associations on which the old faiths depended"; he is a Spencerian *à outrance*. Such a state of mind might be set down as merely belated; but Mr. Holt is anything rather than tardy in his views. My quarrel with him is because, while adhering to the letter of evolution in its strict mechanical form, he would open his mind to the flood of spiritual associations with no sense of the incongruity of such a position. I do not mean to imply that there is anything singular in this procedure, unless it be in the peculiar frankness and honesty of Mr. Holt's ideas. On the contrary, however individual some of his conclusions may appear, he has been borne onward on one of the great tides of the intellect. In the exaltation and lust of conquest that came with the Victorian demonstration of evolution, men's heads were a little turned, and whatever reservations they might make in deference to the Unknowable and the outlying realms of mystery, they were really and pugnaciously convinced that here was the word of truth which should silence the riddling questions of man's soul, as certainly as the Copernican system had led to the untangling of the orbits of the planets. The comparison of Darwin or Spencer with Copernicus became in fact one of the commonplaces of the wise and the unwise.

But this assurance of science was bought at a terrible price. It meant that every appearance of spontaneity in the universe must be subdued to a law of inflexible regularity, and that the soul of man was held to be no more than a momentary centre of molecular force in the vast abyss of matter. Naturally, the imagination of endless space and of the infinite mechanism of time, when the first enthusiasm of assertion calmed down, seemed to the human spirit a chill substitute for

its intuitions of independent existence. In many
thoughtful minds it even awoke a kind of horror,
and the supreme word of Spencer himself, the cod-
icil, so to speak, to his evolutionary testament, is
an ever memorable confession of that feeling:

The thought of this blank form of existence which,
explored in all directions as far as imagination can reach,
has, beyond that, an unexplored region compared with
which the part which imagination has traversed is but
infinitesimal — the thought of a Space compared with
which our immeasurable sidereal system dwindles to a
point, is a thought too overwhelming to be dwelt upon.
Of late years the consciousness that without origin or
cause infinite Space has ever existed and must ever exist,
produces in me a feeling from which I shrink.

Now it is nothing to our purpose here to say
that the notion of infinite space or of any cosmic
mechanism is as purely a piece of self-engender-
ing logic as was Anselm's or any other School-
man's ontological proof of the being of God. The
point is that the hearts of men are never very
brave before the truth, or what they deem the
truth, when their own deeper desires are thwarted.
"The chief component of mind," as Spencer observes, "is feeling," and it is an "enormous error" to suppose that reason, whether right or
wrong, will long endure the attack of our emotions. And so the revulsion from the cruder
dogmas of Victorian materialism has been swift
and sure. In many ways, whether in open rebellion against science or ostentatiously under its

banner, men have turned their eyes once more to

> that true world within the world we see,
> Whereof our world is but the bounding shore —

calling it "true," perhaps, because faith is greater than perception.

Now, outrageous as such a statement may sound, I confess that the conversion of the professional student of science, as, for example, that of Sir Oliver Lodge, has little meaning for me; the very character of his work in investigation seems to have a restricting effect on his mind, so that his sense of the relative value of evidence in other than his own narrow field is likely to be feeble or distorted. But there is deep meaning in the fact that a wary man of the world, who has been imbued with the mechanical theorems of evolution, should yet find this philosophy inadequate to his inner life, and should devote the dearly purchased leisure of his later years to the study of phenomena which, if genuine, must break asunder all the links of Huxley's causal chain and shatter into bits the steadfast cosmic machine of Spencer. For what have cause or calculation to do there where Mr. Holt would take us, even beyond "the region of congruities"? If any one paragraph may be selected as giving the central motive of Mr. Holt's book, it is, I take it, this:

Certain it is that without an abiding consciousness that the known mass of phenomena is not all, and that behind them is a cause transcending our imaginations, life loses some of its best emotions, the imagination grows arid, and the moral impulses shrink. While what we know, and the increasing of it, can more than occupy all our working powers, they work all the better for an occasional dream of greater and less troubled things.

These two bulky volumes, in fact, are essentially the confession of a strong inquisitive mind seeking, under compulsion, to reach some assurance in that "dream of greater and less troubled things." Mr. Holt is one of those who admit that wisdom has come to them by way of sudden conversion. The first warning fell when he was still a young man: "It came," he says, "with the blaze of light, but the light was from the natural sunset which, however, seemed that evening not confined to the far-off clouds, but to pervade the whole atmosphere and all other things, including me, and to be pervaded by energy and mind and sympathy." This, if I interpret his story correctly, was of the preliminary and general sort not unknown in conversions of the more orthodox kind, and needed to be fixed and directed by a later experience. He was turned finally to the new way by a figure and admonition, as he firmly believes, from the other world — an epiphany so dear that he can only hint at it in pious reticence. He had already seen a little of what the commoner sort of mediums can do in furniture-smashing and mind-reading, but now he who — I cannot for-

bear the gentle reproach — can find small time
for Plato, is impelled to give year upon year to
the forty-one volumes of the Proceedings and
Journal of the Society for Psychical Research.
It is not strange that, after this long confinement
and the completion of his great work, his "desire
to get back to the studies of our usual life is like
the desire to get from the fog into the sunlight";
but to some of us his report from that realm of
fog is strange indeed, passing strange.

A considerable part of his book consists of extracts from the publications of the S.P.R., supplemented by a few hitherto unprinted documents
and furnished with a running comment. For the
form in which this material is given us we are
bound to be grateful. The selection includes matter of a later date than that in the *Human Personality* of Mr. Frederic Myers, and is constructed in such a spirit of freedom and fairness
as to justify the reader in feeling that he should
gain little by wading through the enormous mass
of the sources. Nor is Mr. Holt's tone repellently
dogmatic. He admits that he himself is still
groping in these obscure regions, and he does not
hesitate to point out the paradoxical and often
contradictory nature of the evidence. The rôle
of fraud and collusion in the manifestations he
does reject as insignificant and impertinent; and
in this most of us are ready to follow him. No
doubt there has been a vast amount of deliberate

deception in the table-turning and other so-called mediumistic phenomena, but the residue of facts which cannot be accounted for by the ordinary faculties of man is large and presses for explanation. What shall we do with them?

Now a complete Spencerian, and indeed any one who marches under the exclusive flag of science, is bound to hold that these phenomena have their proper place in the scheme of evolution, and so Mr. Holt is at great pains to connect them with the development of man's perceptive powers. I have referred to his eloquent account of the joy of our larger contact with the visible world as compared with the dark and limited horizon of the amœba, from whom man is supposed to be descended. And so analogy suggests to him, as it has suggested to others, that our sensitiveness to "super-usual" phenomena is but the beginning of a new faculty, comparable to the spot on the tegument of the primitive organisms which reacted to a ray of light, and that in time this faculty will be trained to respond to the fulness of the spiritual world as the human eye has grown to embrace the wonders of material vision. The dimness and confusion of psychic perception now are due to our inexperience, and all our knowledge of evolution warrants the hope that some day our children's children shall see with a wide-open inner eye, and shall be able *veras audire et reddere voces*.

Meanwhile not all is darkness. Beyond the incidents of telepathy and telekinesis, which many of the most sceptical of us are beginning to accept, there are those — not the sentimentalists of the old sort, but highly educated men and women — who believe that we already have abundant evidence of true communication with denizens of the other world. Mr. Holt wavers a little when he comes to theorize on these things, but at bottom his conviction is pretty firm that in some way, sometimes obscurely and deceptively, sometimes clearly and commandingly, the dead speak to us through what material mediums they can employ. The "subliminal self" he rejects as a meaningless fiction. In its place he assumes what he calls the Cosmic Soul — the great reservoir from which our mind or spirit emanates, gathers strength and personality by the discipline of life, and then in due time returns to its source, remaining at once a part of the whole and a separate individuality. I can best set forth his views of this delicate matter by quoting three short paragraphs from different parts of the book:

... Indications of a consciousness aware of everything that is going on or has gone on, at least within the sphere of its activity, and which includes and reaches far outside of our activity and our knowledge. All individual consciousnesses seem to be, in some mysterious way, not only themselves, but part of that universal consciousness; for we get from it not only wondrous dream-images of all kinds, but mysterious impressions

from individual consciousnesses other than our own,
which with our own are part of it.

But though perhaps we flow back into this constantly
increasing aggregate of mind — the Cosmic Soul — it
seems much more obviously to flow into us, at times and
in degrees that vary enormously, as we vary. Into the
least sensitive or receptive it does not go perceptibly
beyond the ordinary psychoses of daily life; into others
it seems to penetrate in ways to which we hardly know
how to assign limits. Will it not presumably, as evolution goes on, flow more and more into all of us?

It looks too as if these possibilities might be the supreme justification for the evolution of the universe.
There may be justification enough in birds and flowers,
in the play of lambs and children, in sex, in love, in the
maternity around which so much of the world's worship
has centred, in knowledge, in wisdom, even as they have
been ordinarily understood; but a new significance, a
new joy, a new glory over and beyond them all sometimes seems to have been lately promised by that as yet
dim conception of the Cosmic Soul.

In my small reading in this field I know of no
other expression so clear and persuasive of the
"dream of greater and less troubled things"
which may come to a strong mind from spiritual-
ism. Nothing certainly in Frederic Myers's elegant and learned exposition of the subject has
ever given me the same shock, so to speak, of
veracious experience. Now in one way there is
nothing new in these conclusions. It would be
hard to distinguish between this Cosmic Soul and
that all-embracing Mind with which the Stoic
sought to think in common, as we breathe with

the circumambient air; hard to see how it differs essentially from the *anima mundi* of certain medieval philosophers, or from the Deity of certain half-pantheistic divines — and indeed Mr. Holt does not shrink from calling it by the sacred name of God. Even the attempt to furnish such a belief with a scientific sanction is not altogether unknown, for the Stoic creed was the direct outgrowth of an age of science; but the peculiar kind of confirmation which the devotees of psychical research claim for their hopes from the analogies of evolution is emphatically a new thing. I suspect that the adherence of many "tough-minded" men (as William James would call them), so different from the credulity of the earlier spiritualists, is due in large measure to the illusion of these analogies.

Illusion, I say, for I cannot see one particle of justification for these claims. The publications of the S.P.R. are sufficient evidence that psychic phenomena in these latter years have received a kind of study unknown in the past, and manifestly they have been dislocated into what may seem to be the region of science by the imposition of a classification decked out with the proper furnishing of Greek names. But in essential matters I cannot see the slightest proof of advance in our communication with the other world since the remotest records of history. I can only hint at one or two reasons for my belief, and leave the

argument to the reader to fill out as he may.
Mr. Holt gives several cases of supposed levitation, but is rather doubtful of the facts. Well, if
one will turn to the ancient religious books of
India, one will find that the power of raising the
body into the air is universally taken for granted
as an everyday event. A saint who could not
practise levitation was a mere novice in the
higher life. Did the holy men of India really float
before the eyes of innumerable observers in this
uncanny fashion, and did some of the medieval
mystics enjoy the same sort of privilege? I do
not know; but I am sure that the evidence for the
tradition is as good as most of the tales accepted
by the S.P.R. Again, the trance life was developed
by the ancient Buddhists to a degree, and its
various stages were analysed by them with an
apparatus of scientific terminology, which make
the modern séance seem in comparison the amusement of a spiritual kindergarten. So too the
knowledge of the other world obtained by these
reputable gentlemen was incomparably superior
in scope and precision to any light of recent years.
It would be idle to refer to the records of similar
powers through the classical and middle ages
and in later times, without filling these pages
with examples.[1] Those who are looking for enter-

[1] A quotation from Lactantius (Inst. VII, 13) is sufficient: "Qui [Democritus and the other materialists] pro-
fecto non auderent de interitu animarum mago aliquo

tainment from this subject may be directed to Defoe's *Duncan Campbell*, where, by the way, they will learn that when English was still a living speech, telepathy was merely "a sympathy with souls." And as there is no warrant for asserting any progress in these psychic phenomena, so the hope that some faculty of the soul, now in its primitive state, will develop to wondrous capabilities, is a pure assumption, and cannot be confirmed by analogy with physical evolution. Myers virtually conceded this when he said that the "actual possession and control of human organisms by departed spirits ... carries us back to the most outrageously savage group among the superstitions of the early world." Yet with that sublime indifference to consistency which is the universal mark of pseudo-science, he is ready almost in the same breath to base the certainty of religious faith on our presumed evolution in this direction: "Assuredly this deepening response of man's spirit to the Cosmos deepening round him must be affected by all the signals which now are glimmering out of night to tell him of his inmost nature and his endless fate. Who can think that either Science or Revelation has spoken as yet more than a first half-comprehended word? But if in truth souls departed call to us, it is to them

præsente disserere, qui sciret certis carminibus ciere ab inferis animas et adesse et præbere se humanis oculis videndas et loqui et futura prædicere."

that we shall listen most of all." Alas for the blind hopes and the dark minds of men! How long ago the great evolutionary poet of Rome uttered those words, and these:

> Denique si vocem rerum natura repente
> mittat et hoc alicui nostrum sic increpet ipsa,
> "quid tibi tanto operest, mortalis, quod nimis ægris
> luctibus indulges? quid mortem congemis ac fles?"

That was, and still shall be, the only true consolation, not ignoble indeed, from Nature's voice in the law of evolution. No, these phenomena that transcend the scheme of calculable physical forces, wherever they belong, do not fall within the province of science, and Huxley, though he may have gone too far in denouncing them as gross imposture, was entirely justified as the apostle of evolution in declaring that, even if proved true, they would have no interest for him.

Nor, with the best will in the world, can I see that in themselves they offer any hope of less troubled things in the future. After balancing the evidence with open mind I am bound to say that, in my judgment, it seems to weigh strongly, overwhelmingly, against the hypothesis of communication with the dead. The bulk of the supposed messages from spiritual "controls" are palpably within the natural powers of the medium. Of the few that show knowledge beyond the reach of the medium the majority are easily explained by chance or telepathy, and those that seem to evade this kind of explanation are so extremely rare as scarcely to count at all against the mass of negative arguments; the only safe logic in these exceptional cases is to assume that we are ignorant of some of the circumstances. It is obviously impossible within the compass of an essay to marshal the negative arguments, but one or two of them may be indicated.

In the first place, then, the prearranged tests of a crucial character have failed. "Myers shows lack of memory of languages," says Mr. Holt, "but apparently only where his medium does n't know them; but there's that envelope which he left with Sir Oliver Lodge for the express purpose of giving its contents, and he gave something else! It seems a hopeless muddle of contradictions." I should rather call it a very clear argument. The muddle of contradictions is in the stories which the spirits of wise men and women are believed to send us of life beyond the grave. They say one thing to-day and the very opposite thing to-morrow. When they do not talk nonsense, they commonly talk platitudes. So far as my reading goes, there has never come one single word about the future state, though it be a George Eliot or a Walter Scott who speaks, which goes beyond the imagination of a commonplace or vulgar medium, though, as a matter of fact, some of the unprofessional mediums are refined, intelligent people, when their minds are awake.

This, for instance, is the kind of education that follows us into the other world (George Eliot *loquitur*):

> I being fond, very fond of writers of ancient history, etc., felt a strong desire to see Dante, Aristotle, and several others; Shakespeare, if such a spirit existed. As I stood thinking of him, a spirit instantly appeared, who speaking said, "I am Bacon." ... As Bacon neared me, he began to speak, and quoted to me the following words, "You have questioned my reality. Question it no more. I am Shakespeare."

Nor can I at all follow Mr. Holt in finding an argument for direct possession in the dramatic power of a Mrs. Piper — "more exact and comprehensive," he thinks, "(not more poetic, of course) than that of Shakespeare or Sophocles." I simply cannot see that this power of speaking for various persons surpasses what should be expected from such a medium in the trance state; there seems to me nothing at all miraculous or "super-usual" in it.

Even if it were left a matter of taste, and as such *non disputandum*, to me belief in the genuineness of these "controls" would simply add a new terror to death. Shall there be no escape in this broad universe from folly and ignorance? The believers apologize for the prevalence of these qualities by appealing to the difficulty of establishing communication between those in the spirit and those in the body.[1] I cannot see that

---

[1] It is interesting to observe that Plutarch (*De Pythiæ*

the defence applies. If the communication is established, as they say it is, why should it be harder to give us a bit of real information about the new life than to utter contradictory platitudes? Charles Eliot Norton once had a sitting with Mrs. Piper in the home of William James, and this was the conclusion of his report: "As to the origin of many of the phantasmagorias of her trance dreams, I formed a very distinct opinion, but many experiments would be required to test its correctness, *and these I shall never make*." I hold Mr. Norton's taste to be a deeper wisdom than the unregulated "open-mindedness" of his friend. When the last balance is made up, I even suspect that Mr. James will have been found among the disintegrating and deteriorating forces of the age.

For in its sum this movement, to which Mr. James lent the prestige of his great name, seems to me to lie in a backward direction towards disintegration. As it is not science, so it is not religion. Here is the significant fact. The physical phenomena produced by mediums and "sensitives" are invariably, whether genuine or fraudulent, the work of disorganization and destruction. I have yet to hear of anything constructed or brought into order by the forces of telekinesis,

Oraculis, 21) uses the same apology for the defective wisdom of the oracles given by the dæmon through the organs and incorporated soul of the Pythian medium.

or what not; but I hear of tables foolishly rising into the air, of bells inanely ringing, of guitars smashed, and furniture generally hurled about the room. The literature of the subject has a capital name for the perpetrator of these absurd freaks, the Poltergeist — or demon of confusion — and certainly if there is any god of this world, it is he. Nor does his sway end with material objects, but so far as there is anything super-normal in the spiritual phenomena, here too his mischievous will would seem to be displayed. I do not mean by this that the human soul is chained to a dull mechanic exercise; the word "normal" is not necessarily synonymous with creeping routine. It is possible that in the dream-state there may come to the liberated soul intimations and visions that in one sense quite surpass its normal range, and in deep slumber we may enjoy a foretaste of a divine repose that is by no means the same as sluggish death. I have gone far enough in the old Hindu mysticism to hold my mind open to such beliefs without waiting for confirmation from the reports of modern instances. And these images of the beloved dead that appear to men privately and in secret utter warnings and exhortations of a kind

> to shake our dispositions
> With thoughts beyond the reaches of our souls — .

these, though they be called the creation of fan-

tasy, may yet speak from the deeper wisdom
of the heart, piercing with magic voice through
the crust of diurnal circumstance. Nevertheless,
even here is danger. The critic of literature is
bound to protest against identifying the inspiration of genius too closely with the automatic
creations of the dream-state. That leads straight
to the super-romantic exaltation of Coleridge's
Kubla Khan as the supreme type of poetry, and
to a belittlement of the higher organizing imagination and of the reflective use of experience in
art. Of this sort of criticism we have seen vastly
too much for a hundred years and more. In like
manner we know how the ready hearkening to
"airy tongues that syllable men's names" has
in the past brought many a sturdy mind to credulity and dilapidation. These things we may say
with no lack of deference to those admired names
that have thought, and still think, otherwise.

If I might add another conjecture to the many
that have been thrown out to explain these mysteries, I should say that there may well exist a
great reservoir of free mental and spiritual energy out of which some selective agency within
us has drawn together the stuff of its being and
created what we call our personality, and that in
the same way the universe has its centripetal
will — a deity, a God, men name it — which
shapes about itself a sphere of order and harmony and divine purpose, amid the purposeless

fluctuations of what Plato called the undefined
material of ἀνάγκη, necessity. If this were so,
then the strangely haphazard and insignificant
communications that reach the mind in the
trance state, would be no divine intimations
passing between our soul and the Cosmic Soul, or
World Soul, properly speaking, but would be the
result of suspending the inhibitive force of personality and opening the soul to the influx of
those uncontrolled and unassimilated influences
which stray, as it were, from the fringe and loose
ends of the unseen realm. Glimpses of beauty
may come to the soul by chance in those mo-
ments, and miraculous divinations from the
ragged edge of things, but the outcome at last, if
the mind becomes inured to the medium it works
in, is mental disorganization and spiritual confusion. I remember many years ago hearing a
Presbyterian evangelist, who had once been a
professional spiritualist, discourse on the experi-
ences of his unreformed days. Most of the supernatural phenomena he denounced as pure imposture; but with great earnestness he declared that
there was a residue of mystery which the mediums themselves could not explain, and he warned
his hearers to keep their eyes and ears from meddling with what was manifestly the direct work
of the devil. Well, let us cry peace to the devil.
That august personage is probably too busily
engaged in graver pursuits to be diverted to the

amusements of the séance. But if mythology is to be called in, let us ask rather in wonder why a scholar such as Frederic Myers, who had drunk so deep of the well of Hippocrene, should have turned his attention from Apollo to the Poltergeist? Not here, in the close atmosphere of trance and convulsion —

> Not here, O Apollo!
> Are haunts meet for thee;
> But where Helicon breaks down
> In cliff to the sea.

How then, we ask, has a scholar like Myers or an experienced man of the world like Mr. Holt brought himself to seek comfort in looking at what one of them at least does not hesitate to describe as "a photograph of chaos and old night"? I suspect it is largely through the glamour of a word, the much-repeating of the mystic syllables of "science." The specious analogy with evolution has a power, like charity, to cover the evils of many an inconsistency; and it is probable also that the grandiose achievements of science in the sphere of material motion and change have confirmed the modern mind in a revolt from everything in religion that bears a true or fancied resemblance to quietism. It is, in fact, perilously easy to infer from a philosophy of natural selection that repose and stability are the marks of death and that life and growth are the product of purposeless activity. Hence, in part,

the widespread tendency to honour the tumult
rather than the strength of the soul; and hence,
perhaps, the readiness of men of great intellectual ability to put the Poltergeist in the place
of the old-fashioned God of Providence, whose
commands came to us so persistently in the form
of prohibitions. It is a strange obsession, a stran-
ger faith! If there is any divinity to be learned
from these conclusions of pseudo-science, it
should seem to be the admonition to close the
ears of the spirit to those random calls, whence-
soever they come, and to listen once more for
the still small voice, that was heard thousands of
years ago and is the same to-day as yesterday.
The whisper of the Cosmic Soul so heard may be
only our own soul speaking in the silences of the
flesh — I am not concerned to explain these
things — but its message is clear and certain.
"God," it says, as the great teacher of the Acad-
emy declared, "is a being simple and true both
in act and in word; neither doth He Himself
suffer change nor doth He deceive others by
fantasies or messages or by the sending of signs
whether to the waking or to the sleeping." This
is the same voice that bids us seek the hope of
immortality in the presence of that within us
which amid birth and decay knows itself independent of these and a partaker of the divine
nature; that announces the final grace of happiness in a peace that passes understanding; and

speaks in the life of Socrates and Jesus and ten
thousand other witnesses — but if there, then
not in the words of Spencer or William James.
Why, if a man needs the consolations of religion,
should he seek further than that? Why, if he believes that a verbal revelation is possible, should
he discard the sacred books of mankind for the
fumbling reports of the Society for Psychical Research? And why, in the name of conscience,
why, if a living medium is demanded, is it more
reasonable to suppose that the mystery of life
speaks through Mrs. Piper than through the
Bishop of Rome?

And so, "having laid hands on father Par-
menides," I recoil at my own temerity. The
truth is, in whatever spirit you may take up this
book on the *Cosmic Relations*, its arguments will
impose themselves on you in one way or another
by the sheer weight of the personality behind
them. At least I am sure that, in the very act of
criticising, ignorantly perhaps, its avowedly tentative explanations of psychic phenomena and
the Cosmic Soul, I have felt myself fortified in
my position by a something within the book that
is not tentative at all, but spoken with the authority of certain experience. There are pages
here that any attentive reader will mark for their
pungent expression of knowledge accumulated
from many phases of life; for the privileged few
there are passages of intimate, almost sacred self-

revelation; and then there are other pages for the world in which the S.P.R. is forgotten and the author speaks of immortality and the reasonableness of faith in a way that must arrest the mind of the sceptical materialist and bring courage to the timid believer. If, as I am bound to think, much of the specific theory of the book is drawn from the false usurpations of science, the real motive power behind the arguments is a well-fortified assurance of those greater and less troubled things for which we used to look in places and minds withdrawn from the world. Not many things of recent years are of more significance than that deep intuitions of religion should reach us unmistakably from this source and in the manner of this book. It is not a new thing that a sound intuition should be supported by an untenable theory.

SAMUEL BUTLER OF EREWHON

SAMUEL BUTLER OF EREWHON

It cannot be said that Samuel Butler, the author of *Erewhon* (which is English for Utopia, spelt backwards), was particularly modest as a man or reticent as a writer. Indeed a good part of his published writings are in the form of note-books in which he relates how he acquired his peculiar views on the great questions of the day and how he came to be at loggerheads with the various leaders of contemporary thought. Yet with all that he said little about his personal life, or, rather, he said enough but veiled his confessions in baffling circumlocutions and allegories. From reading his works one got the impression of an impish boy crouching *perdu* behind a stone fence, from which he pelted the citizens on the highway with pebbles and bad words. The situation was made the more piquant by the fact that the good men who were going about their work seemed utterly to disregard the missiles. Now Mr. Festing Jones, the boy's silent partner in mischief, has jerked his comrade into the air, so to speak, and set him up on the wall, as on a pedestal, grimacing visibly there to all the world. Mr. Jones's biography of his friend is no great work of art, but it is an interesting document.

Our Erewhonian's grandfather, another Sam-

uel Butler, was the famous headmaster of Shrewsbury and Bishop of Lichfield, a scholar of some
repute in the good old days when lawn sleeves
were regarded as the natural prize for editing a
Greek tragedy. As a grandfather the grandson
instinctively detested him, until on going through
his ancestor's correspondence for the sake of com-
posing a biography, this feeling was changed to
admiration and fondness. It is a significant fact
that this same biography is the only dull book
he ever wrote; he was a good hater, but a bad
lover. The bishop's son, Thomas, was a solid,
perhaps rather stodgy, clergyman, Rector of
Langar-with-Bramston and Canon of Lincoln,
about whom his Erewhonian son felt no doubt at
all and underwent no conversion. Samuel's portrait of his father in *The Way of All Flesh* is one
of the most elaborately offensive caricatures ever
drawn, and he was capable of writing in a letter:
"My mother is ill — very ill. It is not likely that
she will recover.

> I had rather
> It had been my father."

Which did not mean that he was particularly devoted to his mother. It must be admitted that
Samuel was never dull when he spoke of his
father.

Our Erewhonian, the third of the Butlers whom
we have to mention, was born in 1835. He passed

a wretchedly unhappy childhood at home: if we may believe him and his biographer, because his father was endued with the antiquated Victorian faith in parental authority and with the hateful vices of priestcraft; if we may read between the lines of the record, because Samuel desired from the beginning to be a law unto himself. From home he went to school, first under the Reverend E. Gibson at Allesbey, where he appears to have been equally wretched. At least all we know of him in these days is from a note written in old age on the tedium of divine service.

When I was at school at Allesbey [he says] the boy who knelt opposite me at morning prayers, with his face not more than a yard away from mine, used to blow pretty little bubbles with his saliva which he would send sailing off the tip of his tongue like miniature soap bubbles; they very soon broke, but they had a career of a foot or two. I never saw any one else able to get saliva bubbles right away from him; and though I have endeavoured for some five and fifty years to acquire the art, I never yet could start the bubble off my tongue without its bursting. Now things like this really do relieve the tedium of church.

The story, characteristic in its way of Butler, reminds me of a quip which I once received, written on a postcard, from that exquisite poet, the late Father Tabb:

"Among your many playmates here,
   Why is it that you all prefer
      Your little friend, my dear?"

"Because, mamma, tho' hard we try,
  ;Not one of us can spit so high,
      And catch it in his ear."

Whatever may have been the state of Butler at Allesbey, we have ample evidence of his misery under Dr. Kennedy, his grandfather's successor at Shrewsbury, whither he was sent at the age of twelve. It is enough to say that the school and its master appear in *The Way of All Flesh* as Roughborough and Dr. Skinner.

From Shrewsbury Butler went to St. John's College, Cambridge, where he was happy in a fashion, until he got religion — and then again his troubles began. One may guess from certain passages in *The Way of All Flesh* that he became more deeply involved in the evangelical revival going on among the so-called Johnians than he or his biographer liked to admit in later years. At any rate his purpose at this time was to take orders, and after his graduation he lived for a while as lay assistant to a curate in St. James's Parish, Piccadilly. His work passed among the poor, and was valuable to him no doubt; but Butler at the altar is not conceivable in *rerum natura*, and he soon decided to give up the idea of ordination. His father, of course, threatened to cut off his allowance, and after some correspondence of an unedifying sort it was decided that the son should go out to New Zealand and try his hand at sheep-farming. There his homestead,

called Mesopotamia from its position between
two rivers, "was built upon a little plateau
on the edge of the downs, approached by a cut-
ting from the flat, and was most comfortably
situated and sheltered." With books about him
and his piano, he passed several years in which
active duties were pleasantly combined with contemplation.

It is scarcely too much to say that all the product of his later life was the fruit of this period of
quiet incubation. Here he saturated his imagination with that large majestic scenery which he
was to describe with such splendid effect in
Erewhon. Here he read Darwin's *Origin of
Species*, and got the idea of the evolution of machines which was the germ of so much of his con-
troversial writing. As for his religious beliefs, we
find him reading Gibbon on the outward voyage,
and sending this report to his uncle in England:
"Much as there is in Gibbon which we should
alike condemn — for, however we may admire
his sarcasms, it is impossible not at times to feel
that he would have acted more nobly in suppressing them — he is a grand historian and the impress of a mighty intellect is upon his work."

This from the master of irresponsible sarcasm,
whose talent might almost be said to have been
employed in "sapping a solemn creed with solemn
sneer." A few months later Butler was writing to
a friend: "I think I am a Unitarian now, but

don't know and won't say. As for the Trinity I
cannot make head or tail of it, and feel inclined to
agree with a negro who was heard in church here
the other day repeating the Athanasian creed:
"The Father impossible, the Son impossible, and
the Holy Ghost impossible; and yet there are not
three impossibles, but one impossible." Butler,
we learn from an actual witness, was wrong, for
the coloured preacher's word for the Athanasian
"incomprehensible" was "uncomfortable," not
"impossible"; but accuracy in a jest, Aristotle
would assure us, is not essential to its force as an
argument. The next year Butler was writing, not
in jest but in earnest, that he had renounced
Christianity altogether, being led to that conclusion by difficulties over the Resurrection. Such
at least was his profession at the time; what he
really believed then or at any other time, I should
hesitate to guess, and I doubt if he quite knew
himself.

In 1864 Butler returned to England, with a
mysterious friend named Pauli, whom he supported out of a scanty income, and who swindled
him outrageously. He settled in chambers in
Clifford's Inn, where he lived in a strange isolated
way until his death in 1902. For a number of
years he studied diligently to be an artist, although his talent in that direction was mediocre
if not less. He practised and composed music also,
being a passionate and jealous lover of Handel.

His recreation was travelling in Italy, where he seems to have shown a genial sociability utterly unlike his manners in London.

It is one of the paradoxes of Butler's character that he who theoretically made amiability and charity the chief of virtues and regarded good breeding as the *summum bonum*, who identified the saint with the gentleman and thought the "swell" was the ideal towards which all nature had been groaning and travailing together, — it is a pretty paradox that with such a theory Butler should have been in practice, as he says of himself, "an Ishmaelite by instinct," incapable from the first of adjusting himself to family life, equally incapable of accommodating his habits and temperament to the ordinary demands of society. It may be a nice point in social casuistry whether an Ishmaelite can be a gentleman; apparently Butler proved the combination possible, for with all his cantankerousness — and cantankerous he was with most men and women — one gathers that he bore about him that peculiar stamp of self-respect and directness of manner which mark the gentleman. After all his grandfather was the great doctor of Shrewsbury. Perhaps we should say that the true Englishman alone can combine the qualities of an "original" — *Anglice* for eccentric curmudgeon — and a man of the world; and Butler in every drop of his blood and every fibre of his brain was English.

This is not to say that Butler lived in Clifford's Inn as a bear in his den, entirely without friends. One woman at least broke through the outer barriers of his self-will, though the inner citadel she could not take. At Heatherley's art school Butler became acquainted with a Miss Savage who was painting there in an amateurish way, a plain, sickly, rather dowdy, lonely young woman of his own age. Some congeniality of mind quickly brought them together, and the notes of personal comment and literary criticism that passed between them form the most interesting pages of the biography. Miss Savage may have been physically unattractive, but she was endowed with a wit that approached the diabolical; her letters are a real contribution to English literature. Whether her influence on Butler was entirely beneficial is another question. She gave him the intellectual sympathy and stimulus he needed when all the world was conspiring to neglect him; her advice in matters of detail was shrewd and generally sound; but she flattered outrageously, and her flattery was directed almost exclusively to the side of his work which certainly did not require forcing. The truth is that she understood only the sceptical and sarcastic traits of his mind, while to the deeper vein of poetry in the man and to his spiritual insight—for there was this too in his soul, though much overlaid — she appears to have been quite blind. So long as, to use his own words, he was "heaving bricks into the middle of them," she helped him with ammunition and encouraged him with applause; and if Butler was accoutred to be, as again he says of himself, "the *enfant terrible* of literature and science" and nothing more, he certainly got from her what he needed. But I wonder.

However, if her influence was deleterious, she paid the price. She gave him all, and in return received only a cold friendship of the intelligence. After her death Butler felt something like remorse for this unequal exchange, and docketed and annotated their correspondence in a manner that reminds one of Carlyle's marital repentance. This Butler did, evidently expecting that the letters would one day be published. But he wrote also a couple of terrible sonnets about the poor woman which one hopes he never intended for any other eye than his own. As they are now public, I may quote them for whatever light they throw on the writer's character, and as a specimen of what he might have accomplished in verse.

> She was too kind, wooed too persistently,
> Wrote moving letters to me day by day;
> The more she wrote, the more unmoved was I,
> The more she gave, the less could I repay.
> Therefore I grieve not that I was not loved,
> But that, being loved, I could not love again.
> I liked; but like and love are far removed;
> Hard though I tried to love I tried in vain.

For she was plain and lame and fat and short,
Forty and over-kind. Hence it befell
That, though I loved her in a certain sort,
Yet did I love too wisely but not well.
    Ah! had she been more beauteous or less kind
    She might have found me of another mind.

And now, though twenty years are come and gone,
That little lame lady's face is with me still;
Never a day but what, on every one,
She dwells with me as dwell she ever will.
She said she wished I knew not wrong from right;
It was not that; I knew, and would have chosen
Wrong if I could, but, in my own despite,
Power to choose wrong in my chilled veins was frozen.
'T is said that if a woman woo, no man
Should leave her till she have prevailed; and, true,
A man will yield for pity if he can,
But if the flesh rebels what can he do?
    I could not; hence I grieve my whole life long
    The wrong I did in that I did no wrong.

Among the few male companions of Butler the
primacy must be given to the inimitable Alfred
Cathie, his valet, clerk, guide, philosopher, and
friend. How Alfred happened in real life I do not
know. The creator of Caleb Balderstone might
have made him, or the creator of Sancho Panza
— he is in brief a Caleb and a Sancho combined
and translated into broad Cockney; but how the
good Lord conceived him, I do not know. To
describe him is impossible; I can only transcribe
some of his sayings. Thus, writing to Mr. Jones
he tells of a visit with his master to the Exhibition:

"I enticed Mr. Butler to have a ride with me on it [the Switchback Railway], which he did, but he said when he came off '*it was damnable.*' I soothed him by saying the motion was ridiculous but the sensation was grand." But Alfred did not confine his epistolary talents to absent friends; here, for example, is one of his daily notes of warning and advice to his master:

This is the last notice from Alfred to the effect that Samuel Butler, Esqr. is to buy himself a new Hat on Wednesday morning the 8th of November 1893. Failing to do so there will be an awful scene on his return to Clifford's Inn. — ALFRED.

Of Alfred's autocratic wisdom Butler himself tells this story in a letter:

We have had Venus and Jupiter very bright and very close. One evening they shone clear and near the moon, no other stars being visible. Alfred did not like it, so he said:

"Do you think, Sir, that that is quite right?"

I said I thought it was; but next night the moon was a long way off, so he complained to me and said it was *not* right.

I said: "But you know, Alfred, the moon rises an hour later every night, so it will be an hour yet before it is in the same place."

"Very well, Sir," he answered, finding my explanation a little tedious, "I forgive you this once, but never allude to the subject again in my presence."

But I think the story that pleases me most — it would have brought tears of joy to the eyes of

Charles Lamb — and that best displays Alfred as
a human as well as a celestial philosopher, is this
from Butler's *Note-Books:*

The first time that Dr. Creighton asked me to come
down to Peterborough, in 1894, before he became Bishop
of London, I was a little doubtful whether to go or not.
As usual, I consulted my good clerk, Alfred, who said:
"Let me have a look at his letter, Sir "
I gave him the letter, and he said:
"I see, Sir, there is a crumb of tobacco in it; I think
you may go."
I went and enjoyed myself very much.

The proverb tells us that no man is a hero to
his valet; what shall we say then of a man to
whom his valet is a hero? There must have been
a vein of geniality in Butler somewhere, and he
was, of course, on good terms with one or two
other gentlemen besides his valet and his Boswell
and the Bishop of London; but to society in general he bore himself, I fear, as the well-crusted
curmudgeon I have described him to be. His
silences at a dinner could be awful, and his remarks to a new acquaintance might be atrocious.
That is the paradox of his nature, that he who
made Mrs. Humdrum the arbitress of manners
and morals, as he did in *Erewhon Revisited,*
should have been utterly incapable of the humdrum of social life.

And as Butler was in social intercourse, so he
was in matters of taste. Theoretically his ideal is

the gentleman who has achieved a "charitable inconsistency" and an "amiable indifferentism"; practically he may have been inconsistent, but for charity and amiability and indifferentism — you might as well look for such qualities in Jonathan Swift. To take his *obiter dicta* in literature alone, with the exception of Homer and Shakespeare, whom he admires so far as one can see for the sake of establishing his inconsistency, he rails against almost every settled reputation of past and present times. Dickens's novels are "literary garbage." In Rossetti he can feel only "self-conceit" and "sultry reticence." If brought to book for his opinions he could be as whimsical as he was prejudiced. "No, I don't like Lamb," he used to protest; "you see, Canon Ainger writes about him, and Canon Ainger goes to tea with my sisters." Or he could justify his distaste by means of a sorites that would have made the reputation of ten Aristotelian logicians. Thus: "Blake was no good because he learnt Italian at over 60 in order to read Dante, and we know Dante was no good because he was so fond of Virgil, and Virgil was no good because Tennyson ran him, and as for Tennyson — well, Tennyson goes without saying." He, like other bitter critics, disapproved of criticism and would have nought to do with reviewing, feeling towards that "gay science" much as Dallas did. Yet he possessed one trait which all honest critics will admit to be the goal of their endeavour, the acme of their art, the haven of peace where their weary labour ends — he could condemn without reading. You have heard his pronouncement on Dante; it is printed in the Life on the same page with this beautifully candid admission: "I see Gladstone says he owes all the fine qualities of his mind to the study of Dante. I believe I owe whatever I have to the fact that no earthly power has induced, or ever can induce me to read him." And on another page he swears he never has read, and never will read, Keats or Shelley or Coleridge or Wordsworth; why should he read what he criticizes as bad? This, I take it, is that last refinement of intuition which gives a man a secure place among those unmakers of renown whom Butler's great namesake of *Hudibras* called "the fierce inquisitors of wit."

These are only a few of Butler's dislikes. Nor was his spirit of opposition confined to the winged words of light talk or narrowed to individual reputations. In a moment of candour he declares that he had "never written on any subject unless [he] believed that the authorities on it were hopelessly wrong"; and the authorities happen to have included the philologians entrenched in the universities, the most eminent names in science, and in religion both the orthodox theologians of the Church and the sceptics of the higher criticism. It is not wonderful that he should have exclaimed with a sad pride: "In that I write at all I am among the damned."

His bout with the philologians took place in the lists of Homeric and Shakespearian criticism. To supplant the "nightmares of Homeric extravagance," as he calls them, rightly enough, "which German professors have evolved out of their inner consciousness," he evolved for his part a delicious fancy that the *Odyssey* was composed by a young woman, and that the palace of Odysseus was set by her in her own home in the Sicilian Trapani. I have never met a Greek scholar who would confess that he had even read Butler's work on *The Authoress of the Odyssey;* they prefer the Butlerian canon of condemning without reading. Well, I have perused the book, but I shall neither accept nor condemn. It is uncommonly clever, and the part at least which deals with the question of authorship is amusingly plausible; but the argument, of course, is all based on inference, and does not amount to much more than a *jeu d'esprit*. His other contention in philology, in which he rearranges the order of Shakespeare's Sonnets and builds up a new story of the events underlying them, should, I feel, be taken rather more seriously. I would not say that, in my judgment, he has made out his case; for here again the evidence is too inferential, too evasive, to be thoroughly conclusive. But I do think that he has demolished the flimsy theories of Sidney

Lee and certain other so-called authorities, and that his own constructive criticism is worthy of attention.

But these tilts with the entrenched philology of the universities were mere skirmishes, so to speak; the real battle was with the authorities in science and theology. These were the gentlemen, "hopelessly wrong," whom Butler undertook to set right by the genial art of "heaving bricks." In science the great enemy was none other than Darwin himself, with all those who swore by the name of Darwin. The dispute did not touch the fact of evolution itself, for Butler to the end was a staunch evolutionist; nor did it concern the Darwinian theory of the survival of the fit, for here again Butler was thoroughly orthodox. The question at issue was the cause of those variations out of which the more fit were selected for survival — and this, I take it, is still the *casus belli* which renders the resounding warfare of the biologists so amusing a spectacle to one who has set his feet in the serene temples of scepticism, whence, as the old Roman poet says, who was yet himself so deeply engaged in the fray —

> Despicere unde queas alios passimque videre
> Errare atque viam palantis quærere vitæ.

On the one side stood in array the host of Darwinians — or ultra-Darwinians, for Darwin himself was provokingly muddled and inconsistent in his statements — who held that the *via vitæ* was a path of incalculable hazard, to whom life was pure mechanism and evolution meant a transference to biology of the mathematical law of probability. On the other side, in which for some time Butler was almost the sole champion in England, stood those who believed that the significant variations arose from the purposeful striving of individual creatures to adapt themselves to their surroundings, and that the selective power of fitness was part of a grand design working itself out consciously in the evolution of life.

Now it is not my business to pronounce judgment in so learned a dispute; the non-scientific critic who should presume to come between such quarrelsome kinsfolk would probably fare like the proverbial peacemaker between man and wife. I can only say that to Butler the dignity of science and the very issues of life seemed to be involved in the debate: "To state this doctrine [of the Darwinians]," he declares, "is to arouse instinctive loathing; it is my fortunate task to maintain that such a nightmare of waste and death is as baseless as it is repulsive." Butler's particular contribution to the Lamarckian side was what he called "unconscious memory," the theory, that is, that the acquired experience of the parent was passed on to the embryo and carried by the offspring into life as an instinctive propensity. Later he learned that the same theory had been propounded by an Austrian biologist named Hering, and thereafter he was careful to ascribe full credit to his predecessor.

The contest unfortunately was embittered at an early stage by a blunder on the part of Charles Darwin and a misunderstanding on the part of Butler. In February of 1879 Ernst Krause, a German scholar, published in *Kosmos* an article on Erasmus Darwin and his Lamarckian brand of evolution. In May of the same year appeared Butler's *Evolution Old and New*. Then, in November, Murray issued a translation of Krause's monograph, under the title of *Erasmus Darwin*, with a preliminary notice by Charles Darwin. Now between the printing of Krause's original essay in February and the publishing of the translation in November, Darwin had sent the author a copy of Butler's book, with the advice that he, Krause, in revising his work, need "not expend much powder and shot on Mr. Butler, for he really is not worthy of it." Accordingly, in reworking his essay for the English translation, Krause made a contemptuous allusion to Butler without naming him. Then for his preface to the translation Darwin first wrote a paragraph beginning with the words: "Dr. Krause has taken great pains and has largely added to his essay since it appeared in *Kosmos*." But, finding this paragraph otherwise irrelevant, Darwin struck it out, without inserting anywhere else a notice of Krause's revision of the work. Hence to Butler, comparing the original German text with the English, it appeared that the version of an article written before the publication of his book contained an insulting reference to that book. Naturally he was incensed, believing that the translator and Darwin had dishonestly insinuated this reference into the work they were pretending to translate literally. To make matters worse, Darwin, on the advice of Huxley and against the advice of his sons, refused to issue any public rectification of the error. In this way a note of personal acrimony entered into Butler's part in the controversy; and this was not mollified by his belief that the Darwinians tried to discredit him by a conspiracy of silence, which extended to suppressing in the reviews any notice even of works foreign to the actual controversy. It may be said for Butler that at least some of the later biologists adopted his views while contemptuously refraining from naming him. Such petty jealousies, it is sad to admit, do perturb the quiet walks of professional scholarship.

But I hasten to descend from the aërial heights of pure science to a region where the critic of letters may feel that he is walking with his feet on the ground. The notable fact is that Butler's whole literary career took its start from his interest, at first merely amateurish, in the Darwinian theory of evolution. Readers of *Erewhon* will remember the three chapters of that Utopian romance entitled *The Book of the Machines*. These chapters stand out as the most brilliant section of the romance; they are furthermore the germ out of which the whole narrative grew, and in a way strike the key-note of much of his later writing. No one, I think, can read this *Book of the Machines* without feeling that it is the work of a powerful and original intellect, but one is likely also to lay it down with a sense of bewilderment. There is insight here, the insight of a mind brooding on the course of human history and speaking with apparent sincerity of a terrible danger to be avoided. Yet there is withal a note of biting irony; and what precisely the object of this irony may be, or how this irony is to be reconciled with the tone of sincerity, the book itself gives one no clue to determine.

Nor do the author's direct allusions to his purpose give us much ease. In a letter to Darwin accompanying a present of the first edition of *Erewhon*, in 1872, Butler disclaims any intention of being "disrespectful" to the *Origin of Species*, and avows that the chapters on Machines, written primarily as a bit of pure fun, were rewritten and inserted in *Erewhon* as a satire on the pseudo-scientific method of Bishop Butler's *Analogy*. Again, in the preface to the second edition of the book published a few months after the first, he expresses his "regret that reviewers have in some cases been inclined to treat the chapters on Machines as an attempt to reduce Mr. Darwin's theory to an absurdity." He is surprised that the specious misuse of analogy really aimed at should not have occurred to any reviewer. Evidently he is alluding again to Bishop Butler, yet if one turns to page 84 of the narrative itself, one sees that Paley's famous analogy of the watch, and not Bishop Butler at all, was in the author's mind when he wrote the book. This is already a little confusing, but confusion is worse confounded by the statement in a letter written shortly before our Erewhonian's death. Now, looking back at the matter through the bitterness engendered by what he regarded as a long persecution, he says: "With *Erewhon* Charles Darwin smelt danger from afar. I knew him personally; he was one of my grandfather's pupils. He knew very well that the machine chapters in *Erewhon* would not end there, and the Darwin circle was then the most important literary power in England."

Here is a beautiful case for genetic criticism — if the word "genetic " has any meaning outside of the dictionary and the laboratory — and by following the development of Butler's ideas one may learn perhaps how the baffling mixture of irony and sincerity got into the famous chapters on Machines and became a kind of fixed habit with him. Darwin's *Origin of Species* reached Butler in New Zealand soon after its publication, and evidently quite carried him off his feet. Under the first spell of admiration he composed a little essay on *Darwin Among the Machines*, which was printed in the *Press* of Canterbury, New Zealand, in 1863. Years later, commenting in one of his scientific books on this article, he admits that he had taken Darwin at his face value without much reflection; "there was one evolution" for him then, and "Darwin was its prophet." And the article itself fully bears out this statement. Caught by the plausible simplicity of evolution as an extension of purely inorganic law into the organic world, Butler carried the mechanical analogy a step further and undertook to show what would happen when machines had progressed to the stage of independent racial existence and had surpassed man, just as the animal kingdom had been evolved out of the vegetable, and the vegetable from the mineral. His conclusion is "that war to the death should be instantly proclaimed against them. Every machine of every sort should be destroyed by the well-wisher of his species. . . . Let us at once go back to the primeval condition of the race."

It must be remembered that Butler wrote this essay while living in the free primitive uplands of New Zealand, during the happiest period of his life, and that the note of primitivism in his peroration is probably in large measure sincere. At the same time there is a word in his later comment which points to another trait in his intellectual make-up which was active from the beginning. He started, he says, with the hypothesis of man as a mechanism, because that was the easiest strand to pick up, and because "there was plenty of amusement" to be got out of it. Now one may amuse one's self with a theory which one holds in all sincerity; but fun of that sort has a way of running into irony or sarcasm, and so one may detect in this first essay the germ of Butler's later manner. He was ever prone to make fun, and sometimes a very strange sort of fun, when he was most in earnest.

It is clear that Butler was both attracted and teased by Darwin's great work, and that he did not rest with his first impression. Two years later, having meanwhile returned to England, he sent another letter to the Canterbury *Press*, which he entitled *Lucubratio Ebria* and signed with a different name. "It is a mistake, then," he says in this second letter, "to take the view adopted by a previous correspondent of this paper." His thesis now is that machines are really an extension, so to speak, of a man's limbs, of the tools, that is to say, which the mind invents in its progress towards a higher organization; as such the development of machinery is the measure of an inner growth and need not be feared.

As yet, apparently, the fun of the thing was still uppermost in Butler's mind. He put the two essays together as *The Book of the Machines* and wrote his Utopian romance about them without feeling any serious discordance in the points of view, and could even send the volume to Darwin with an assurance of his loyalty. But the rift was already there. As he continued to reflect on the matter, the significance of the second point of view took on more importance and he began to see its scientific implications. Out of these reflections grew his book on *Life and Habit* (1877), in which he first, frankly and definitely, announced himself as a champion of the teleological theory of evolution against the mechanistic principles of the ultra-Darwinians.

But our concern now is with the fact that in the latest, revised edition of *Erewhon* the two essays on machines, though much enriched and enlarged in the process of revision, still lie side by side, with no word to tell the reader which of the two represents the author's real views. The result is piquant to say the least. In one chapter the dread of machines, as they have been developed to a state of almost independent consciousness, is expressed with a depth of conviction that can leave no doubt of the author's sincerity. Here he speaks as a Darwinian *à outrance*, but as a Darwinian filled with loathing for the spectres conjured up by his own science. Yet turn a few pages, and you will find machines glorified "as a part of man's own physical nature," the instruments by which alone he advances in "all those habits of mind which most elevate [him] above the lower animals":

Thus civilization and mechanical progress advanced hand in hand, each developing and being developed by the other, the earliest accidental use of the stick having set the ball rolling, and the prospect of advantage keeping it in motion. In fact, machines ought to be regarded as the mode of development by which human organism is now especially advancing, every past invention being an addition to the resources of the human body.

What is one to make of this flagrant contradiction? I might answer by asking what one is to make of the contradictions of life. It is true that the progress of civilization seems to be coincident with mechanical invention. We believe that; and yet can any one look at the state of the world to-day, at the monotony of lives that have been enslaved to machinery, at the distaste for work and the unrest of the worker that have arisen partly as a consequence of this subservience, can any one seriously contemplate the growing materialism of modern life, its dependence for pleasure on the whirl of wheels and the dance of images, with its physical distraction and its lessening care for the quiet and ideal delights of the intellect — can any one see these things and not feel a stirring of something like terror in the soul at the tyranny of the creatures we have evoked from the soulless forces of nature? Life is a dilemma, and only the fool thinks it is simple. In *The Book of the Machines* one of its enigmas is presented with a keenness of observation and a cogency of style that must give the author a high place among the philosophical writers of the age.

However Butler may have been disposed towards the evolution of machines, the Erewhonians themselves chose to see in them a menace to humanity, and decreed that they should be ruthlessly destroyed. *Erewhon* is thus the story of a people who are living backwards, so to speak, of a country seen through the looking-glass and conceived in the spirit of irony. There is no doubt of this intention, you will feel it on every page of the romance; only, and this is the tantalizing spell of the book, it is not always easy to guess against whom the irony is directed. We know from Butler's statement elsewhere, not from the book itself, that the account of the Erewhonian treatment of crime as a disease to be cured in hospitals and of disease as a crime to be punished in prisons was meant to be taken *au pied de la lettre*, and that the law of *Erewhon* was commended by way of satirizing the law of England. But no sooner has the reader adjusted his mind to this form of attack than he finds himself engaged in that terrible arraignment of the Church as working through the so-called Musical Banks, where the Erewhonians themselves become the object of irony. And so the satire sways this way and that from chapter to chapter. It is all good fun, but it is mighty bewildering unless one comes to the book with a knowledge of Butler's ideas derived from other sources; and even then one does not always know on which side of the mouth to laugh — though of the laughter there is never any doubt. The fact is that irony had become a habit with Butler, and of its application he little recked. He could even believe he was ironical when in truth he was perfectly sincere; which is still more delightfully puzzling than his ambiguous application of irony.

This trait comes out in his treatment of Christianity. He had early become interested in the problem of the Resurrection of Christ as the corner-stone of the whole dogmatic edifice, his own sober conclusion apparently being that Christ did not die on the Cross, but was buried while in a trance, and afterwards appeared actually in the flesh to the disciples. His first thoughts on the question were published in a pamphlet, now quite forgotten; and late in life he wrote his *Erewhon Revisited*, which is nothing less than an elaborate and vicious satire, in rather bad taste, on the miraculous birth and the Ascension. But between these two publications comes *The Fair Haven*, as enigmatical a work as ever was penned. Here the problem of the Resurrec-

tion is discussed by a priest, who, having fallen
into scepticism, finds for himself at last a haven
of peace in the solution of every doubt. Now, for
all that one can learn from Butler's life, the solution offered by his fictitious hero was intended to
be taken ironically, and the whole treatise should
be regarded as a diatribe against Christian dogma.
To his friend, Miss Savage, it is "sanglant satire," and so apparently it appeared to Mr. Jones.
Very well; but what really happened? The book
was reviewed in several of the Evangelical peri-
odicals of the day as perfectly orthodox, and so
alert a critic as Canon Ainger sent it to a friend
whom he wished to convert. And to-day a candid reader, even with full knowledge of Butler's
avowed intention, is likely to close the book with
an impression that, despite a note of irony that
breaks through the language here and there, the
argument as a whole forms a singularly powerful
and convincing plea for Christianity. The hallu-
cination theory of the Resurrection propounded
by Strauss is analysed and refuted with remorse-
less logic. Even the trance theory, which Butler
himself was inclined to accept, is answered, briefly
indeed, but plausibly. On the other side Dean
Alford's half-hearted attempt to reconcile the
discordant Gospel narratives of the Resurrection
undergoes the same deadly analysis. But the
truth of the Resurrection, Butler then argues, is
dependent on no such reconciliation of the rec-

ords; in fact a divine revelation, he maintains, designed for the needs of all sorts and conditions of men, ought, in the nature of the case, to present the truth in a variety of manners. Here at last one begins to feel that the satire of Christianity itself is coming out into the open, and in the Life a bit of conversation is recorded which would seem to confirm such a view. Butler is talking with the Rev. Edwin A. Abbott:

He said to me: "And did you really mean none of that part seriously?"

I said: "Certainly not; I intended it as an example of the kind of rubbish which would go down with the *Spectator*."

Abbott said: "Well, I can only say you would have found a great many to sympathize with you, if you had meant it seriously."

I said, rather drily: "That, I think, is exceedingly probable," meaning that there was no lack of silly insincere gushers.

That has a categorical ring; yet in an article (*Essays on Life, Art, and Science*, p. 137) published in the *Universal Review* four years after the date of this conversation, where there can be no possible suspicion of irony, Butler is repeating as his own this same argument for the adaptability of revelation and of the Christ-Ideal.

What can we make of all this? The key to the difficulty may be found, I think, in a sentence of his preface to *The Fair Haven:* "I was justified," he says, "in calling the book a defence — both as against impugners and defenders," i.e., of Christianity. Butler held it his mission to "heave bricks" at two groups of eminent men: he was himself deeply immersed in science, but he nursed a magnificent grudge against the professional scientists of his day both for their bigotry and for personal reasons; and in like manner he was interested in religion and indeed always called himself a churchman of a sort, but he hated any one else who assumed that name. And so in *The Fair Haven* he was having his fun — and powerful good fun it is — with Strauss and the scientific impugners on the one side, and with Dean Alford and his tribe of puzzled defenders on the other; he enjoyed the sport so much that he persuaded his friend and almost made himself believe that he was having fun also with the object impugned and defended by them. But besides the faculty of irony Butler possessed in equal measure the faculty of hard logic. And so it happened that when he came to present the case in support of Christianity any lurking intention of irony was soon swallowed up in the pure delight of building up a constructive argument such as the professional champions of the Church, in his opinion, had quite failed to offer. He was helped in this by his firm belief that of the two the professors of science were a more bigoted and dangerous class than the professors of religion.

In this union of logic with irony Butler belongs

with Huxley and Matthew Arnold, as he is their peer in the mastery of a superbly clear and idiomatic English style. He differs from them in that he possessed also a certain gnome-like impudence of fancy which led him into strange ambiguities and throws a veil of seeming irresponsibility over much, not all, of his writing. Readers who are not made uneasy by this remarkable combination of qualities, and who have no fear for their own heads where brickbats are flying, will find in him one of the most fascinating authors of the Victorian age. Only, perhaps, a word of caution should be uttered in regard to Butler's one regular novel, *The Way of All Flesh*. There is no irony here, but the bludgeoning of a direct and brutal sarcasm; he is no longer our Victorian Swift of *A Tale of a Tub* or of *Laputa*, but a voyager to the land of the Yahoos. It is a powerful book, even a great book in a way; but it is bitter, malignant, base, dishonourable, and dishonest. Unfortunately, to the smudged and smeared minds of a Bernard Shaw and a Gilbert Cannan it appeals as Butler's masterpiece, and much of his fame, so far as he is known to the general public, derives from Shaw's eulogy of this one work. That is a pity, in my judgment; for the true Butler, perhaps I should say the finer Butler, is not there, but in the books where irony plays waywardly backwards and forwards through a network of subtle logic.

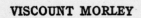

VISCOUNT MORLEY

VISCOUNT MORLEY

"THE world," says Lord Morley in the introduction to his *Recollections*, "is travelling under formidable omens into a new era, very unlike the times in which my lot was cast." And, indeed, those of us who had our beginnings in the Victorian age seem, as we read his pages, to hear a voice out of our own youth, speaking to us almost as strangers — so hard is it for a man in the season of harvest to recall the days of his sowing. That is the deeper meaning of the book. Of the ordinary intimacies of biography it contains small measure. Save for a few sentences about his parents in the first chapter, and the casual mention of "my wife," the writer might be regarded as a modern Melchisedec, "without father, without mother, without descent." Nor has he much to say of his own more private emotions, of the sweet and bitter currents of self-approval and self-distrust that flow through the heart when the world is shut out. In that respect we may call his taste impeccable or his intellect cold, as our judgment inclines. But of the other ingredients of good biography there is abundance. Everywhere there is felt the charm of a writer who has borne a great rôle among great men, and who

knows how to wield all the necromantic devices
of literary art.

No small part of the record is purely bookish,
the reflections of a man who began life as an
author and through all the distractions of a public
career never forgot the seclusions of his library.
There was in Morley the making, perhaps the
actuality, of a first-rate critic, in the narrower
sense of the word, and the interest of these critical
comments is enhanced by the fact that much of
it relates to writers whom he knew personally,
often intimately. No finer tribute to the over-
flowing courage of Meredith, "his spaciousness of
mind and outlook," will be found anywhere than
in these pages. What, for instance, could be more
significant than this extract from a letter of Meredith's written after Morley had called his attention to Goethe's psalm of life, *Das Göttliche?* —
"Anything grander than the days and nights at
my porch, you will not find away from the Alps,
for the dark line of my hill runs up to the stars,
the valley below is a soundless gulf. There I pace
like a shipman before turning in. In the day,
with a S.W. blowing, I have a brilliant universe
rolling up to me; after midnight I sat and thought
of Goethe, and of the sage in him and the youth."
That, as Morley adds, is Meredith as he lived,
and at his best. Yet, as a critic, Morley was not
blind to the strain of contortion in Meredith's
genius, and to what such contortion means. "It

is of no avail," he says, "for any writer to contend that he is not obscure.... The truth is that Meredith often missed ease. Yet ease in words and artistic form has been a mark of more than one of his contemporaries, who amid the world's riddles saw deepest and felt warmest. Even into his best talks there came now and again a sense of strain; if a new-comer joined the little circle of intimates, he was transformed, forcing himself without provocation into a wrestle for violent effects." It would be well if the implication of these words were remembered not only by the over-zealous partisans of Meredith, particularly of Meredith the poet, but by all those would-be "intellectuals" who measure the wisdom of an author by his difficulty.

Space would fail if I undertook to recall the judgments of like clarity passed on R. L. Stevenson and Matthew Arnold and Leslie Stephen and Browning and other lights of the Victorian age. Only one of the greater names is conspicuous by its absence; Thackeray is nowhere even named. I have inquired whether there was any personal reason for this strange silence, but no one has been able to explain it on such grounds. And so I can only fall back on the suggestion of a very wise friend, that Morley may have been repelled by the novelist's insight into the vanities of the human heart, and made uneasy by the realism of the social ideas expressed in the conversation between

Pendennis and Warrington. That is mere conjecture, but there are, in fact, sentences in the talk of those observers of the Upper Temple which might strike as a chilling wind on the illusions of a sentimental Liberal.

But the literature of the *Recollections* is not confined to contemporary writers. To the end, Morley carries on the love of the Classics which came to him, we may suppose, by right of his Oxford training. Late in life, when released for a while from business, he finds more refreshment from a treatise of Cicero than from the daily press. And one of the best of his chapters is really an independent essay in little on Lucretius, to whom, as to the greatest of those who have "denied divinely the divine," he was peculiarly drawn. It is even characteristic of his reserve that nowhere else do we seem to get so near a glimpse into his own more intimate thoughts as in his lingering reflections on the lines of the *De Rerum Natura* which describe the inroad of death upon the pleasant customs of life:

It was impossible that our own glorious literature should not contain, in prose and verse alike, a thousand things of superlative beauty about this universal theme, from Raleigh's "*O eloquent, just, and mighty death,*" or the thrilling dialogues in Claudio's prison, down to the most melting and melodious single verse in all the exercises of our English tongue, "*After life's fitful fever he sleeps well,*" the tender summary of it all. Still, the famous passage of Lucretius at the close of his third book is of such quality that I hardly find in my heart to quarrel with the accomplished critic of to-day who suggests that "its lofty passion, its piercing tenderness, the stately roll of its cadences, is perhaps unmatched in human speech."

Death is the tritest of events save only birth, and the world, it should seem, has agreed to debar it from further exploitation in literature, as a theme long ago exhausted. Yet in this same chapter — the record of an Easter holiday spent in turning over a volume of collectanea on *les grands hommes qui sont morts en plaisantant* — Lord Morley has prefaced his criticism of Lucretius with a sheaf of quotations from English sources which might make the act of dying appear as a new experience to each of us. I will not apologize for writing out two of these extracts; for the more personal flavour of Lord Morley's book is in these things, and still, despite our modern convention of silence, death is closer to our minds than any man.

QUEEN ELIZABETH. (*Philosophy of the man of action.*) — As for me, I see no such great reason why I should either be proud to live, or fear to die. I have had good experience of this world. I have known what it is to be a subject, and I now know what it is to be a sovereign. Good neighbours I have had, and I have met with bad; and in trust, I have found treason. I have bestowed benefits on ill deservers; and where I have done well, I have been ill reputed and spoken of. When I call to mind things past, behold things present, and look forward to things to come, I *count them happiest that go hence soonest.* Nevertheless ... I am armed with better courage than is common in my sex, so that whatsoever befalls me, death shall never find me unprepared.

LEIGHTON. (*The Scotch divine of the time of the Restoration, indifferently episcopal and presbyterian, the friend of Bishop Burnet who reports this of him.*) — There were two remarkable circumstances in his death. He used often to say that if he were to choose a place to die in, it should be an inn, it looking like a pilgrim's going home, to whom this world was all an inn, and who was weary of the noise and confusion of it. He added that the officious tenderness of his friends was an entanglement to a dying man, and that the unconcerned attendance of those that could be procured in such a place would give less disturbance. He had his wish.

In comparison with the point and variety of the literary comments the narrative of Lord Morley's political career is, it must be admitted, rather monotonous. I do not mean that these chapters are wholly without interest. Here and there they are enlivened by sprightly anecdote, as when he tells the story of the Irish peasant in the dock for a violent assault. — *Prisoner,* puzzled by the legal jargon of the indictment: "What's all that he says?" *Warder:* "He says ye hit Pat Curry with yer spade on the side of his head." *Prisoner:* "Bedad, an' I did." *Warder:* "Then plade not guilty." All this aloud and in full hearing of the court. — We may be grateful to an Irish Secretary for assuring us that one of the ancient phantoms of Hibernian humour was a real creature of flesh and blood; it is in a small way a footnote to the veracity of history. There are also in these political chapters several set character sketches of statesmen — notably of Harcourt, Rosebery, Chamberlain, and Lord Spencer — which are scarcely less elaborately drawn than the literary portraits. Nevertheless, the main narrative, when it gets caught in the backwash of Home Rule and Indian administration, moves with a provokingly sluggish tide. Here Lord Morley contrives to be almost as dull about himself as he was about Gladstone in that biography of which he has been heard to say that no one ever read it through.

Yet, withal, it is true that the main, or at least the final, interest of the *Recollections* is drawn from this political background. In telling his story Lord Morley makes rather a sharp division between his hours in Parliament and the hours spent among his books. Such an arrangement would suggest rather an incompatibility between the two parts of his life than their harmony. And so, in fact, after relating his election to Parliament, he pauses a moment to reckon up the difficulties that have beset the literary man in politics, beginning with Cicero, who came to a bloodstained end on the Italian seashore, and closing with Thiers, who used to say that "he would willingly give the writing of ten successful histories for a single happy session in the Assembly

or a single fortunate campaign in arms." But
certainly the reader of Lord Morley's life feels no
such difficulties; on the contrary, he is charmed
by the apparently easy blending of fine culture
with practical success. Perhaps we are the more
sensitive to the beauty of this delicate adjustment
for the reason that in its perfection it is not likely
soon to appear again. We shall, no doubt, continue to see literary men engaged in politics, but
scarcely of Lord Morley's type; and even if such
appear, their literature will be a thing rather held
apart, easily forgotten when they stand in Parliament before the representatives of the people,
or when they are talking business in private with
their colleagues. At least the habit of the Classics, linking the senate with the schoolroom and
associating the problems of to-day with the long
tradition of experience, is passing, or has passed,
away.

Somewhere Lord Morley tells of a conversation with Harcourt when it was a question of letting Home Rule fall into the limbo of pious opinions or of pressing it to a quick and perhaps haz-
ardous issue. Harcourt was for postponement,
and one of the strongest incentives Morley could
bring for action was the appeal of three lines
of Virgil. "Harcourt," he observes, "could be
trusted in passing to forgive desperate politics for
the sake of a classic quotation." In another
place he imagines a debate between Harcourt and

Fox, in which the elder statesman expounds his well-known theory that if a man's aim is public speaking, Euripides ought to be his constant study, scarcely less than Homer himself. (Ah, if one could have been present at such a meeting, and could have been allowed to put in a word for Thucydides as the master statesman of them all!) And the reply is that Homer and Euripides alike have long followed the power of the Crown. "Never again," adds the recorder of the imaginary scene — "never again will either House hear a Minister declaim the solemn hexameters of Lucretius, among the noblest in all poetry; or the verses where Virgil describes the husbandman turning up with rake and plow the rusty javelins, empty helms, and mighty bones of a forgotten battle-field of long ago; or like Pitt in his glorious speech against the Slave Trade, inspired by the shooting of a beam of the rising sun through the windows of the House to the most beautiful and apt of recorded parliamentary impromptus in the two Latin lines:

> Nos ... primus equis Oriens afflavit anhelis,
> Illic sera rubens accendit lumina Vesper."

These are but pretty customs, the practical man may say, the frippery and baubles of political life, which only the dilettante will regret much to see stripped off. Does human welfare depend on the memory of a few scraps of Latin? The matter is not so simple as that. The disappearance of the ancient habit, as Lord Morley himself acknowledges, is "significant of a great many more important things than a casual change in literary taste"; it means a new kind of men in the seats of authority, a new sort of life as the aim of government, a new standard of morality, other hopes and other prizes, a world set free from its moorings. The change began with the Reform Bill of 1832; it was a revolution by the time the century closed; its fruits, whether bitter or sweet, our children shall eat. Lord Morley speaks of Harcourt as the last of the line of orators and lawmakers, great from Somers and Sir Robert Walpole onwards, who, one might add, like the riders seen by Socrates in the Piræus, carried lighted torches which they passed from one to another as they raced through the night. The reader of these memoirs will probably think of Lord Morley himself as the last of the bearers of the torch. When that light has flickered out, will the dawn have come, or will it be only darkness?

Of this revolution which has been going on under our eyes Lord Morley was sufficiently aware, as may be known from the sentence of his Introduction already quoted in this essay. But it is not clear — and this is the question that has constantly intrigued us while reading the *Recollections* — whether he really ever stopped to reflect on his own ambiguous position in the movement. That absorption in the great literary tradition, especially the vivid reality of the Classics which has formed so large a part of the consolation and dignity of his life, and has made him a citizen of the world of Ideas whilst engaged in the pursuits of time — what is this but the fine flower of his Oxford training? And it is incontrovertible that Oxford, whatever the disadvantages or virtues of its discipline, is, and was to a much greater degree when Morley went up, a creation of the Church. Take away the influence of those priests, whose semi-seclusion from present affairs threw them back upon the past, and whose study of the Christian Fathers was curiously blended with reverence for the earlier antiquity of paganism, and you have taken away the very spirit of the place. I am not unaware of the paradox inherent in the age-long coördination of Aristotle with Saint Paul, nor do I believe that a truly classical education is necessarily dependent on the maintenance of such a paradox; but it is a fact nevertheless that the culture of Oxford was, and essentially still is, of this sort, a working compromise between the authority of the Church and the liberty of ancient literature; to discredit the one has been to weaken the other. Now if Morley had seen the intricacy of this compromise and had sought to justify it or with tender touch to readjust its members, or if he had cast away both elements together as rubbish, one could understand his motives, whether one approved or disapproved. But he nowhere hints that he was even conscious of such a problem, and one is left to feel in his attitude towards his intellectual nurse something that smacks of mere disloyalty. The few paragraphs on his undergraduate days are the shabbiest thing in the book. He does not deny the spell of "antique halls and gray time-worn towers" — his whole autobiography would prove his sensitiveness to such a spell, had he not expressly acknowledged it — but at the close of his career, as he looks back on those days, it seems as if the only intellectual matter that seriously concerned him then was the spread of Liberal principles as they percolated into the university from the writings of John Stuart Mill. His scant gratitude to the real *genius loci* has not even the dignity of Gibbon's outspoken contempt. And after that, if one stops to think, there is something disquieting in the cold and calculating purpose of his life to undermine the religious faith of Oxford while continuing to indulge himself in the glamour of her hoarded literary faith. It were better to feel the power of Lucretius and still to believe in God, as the Oxford priests had been content to do, than to be blind, as Morley seems to be, to the subtle complexity of the forces that moulded his taste. A positivist who loves Plato, after the manner of Mill and Morley, is a harsher paradox than ever held the heart of the charmed city by the Isis.

And Morley's acceptance of the finer pleasures of society is of a piece with his ingratitude towards the source of his culture. It would be hard to name a recent book that brings us into higher company than do these *Recollections*. Considering the humbleness of the author's origin — he was the son of an insignificant Lancashire surgeon — one might be tempted to regard his relish of noble names as a sign of snobbishness. But it is nothing of the sort. He moved among the best of the land because by taste and character and achievement he was one of them. His easy familiarity with men born into the ruling caste, if any criticism is to be pronounced, is rather an apology for the existence of such a caste than an indication of subservience on his part. But that is a question beside the point. We are only concerned with his unconcealed delight in the inherited manners of great families and in the decorum of great houses. No Tory of them all could show a franker appreciation of the political advantages coming by natural right to a man like Lord Houghton, now Lord Crewe, from a father "of singular literary and social mark." With such a colleague he admits that he found it easy to work harmoniously. And he is equally sensitive to the grace of noble surroundings. He was never, we may suppose, much attracted to Disraeli's tinselled splendours, but there is no note of disapprobation when to the account of an evening in the magnificent library of Althorpe he adds: "Like a scene from one of Dizzy's novels, and all the actors men with parts to play." Still more characteristic perhaps is his record of two visits to Lord Rosebery. "Meanwhile," he says of one of these, "the upshot of our various talks as we drove, or strolled about Epsom Downs, or chatted in the library, was something of this kind: — The triple alliance (Harcourt, himself, and me) — so much more really important, as I said, laughing, than that of the Central Powers — to remain on its proposed footing." From the account of the second visit I may quote at greater length:

Later and after tea we had an hour's drive, and then at 8:30 we had dinner served under the verandah in the garden. Reminded me of a dinner I once had at Berchtesgaden with Chamberlain years ago. Only we had now a perfect service, instead of two German waiters attending on twenty miscellaneous people, screaming and being screamed at by an overdriven cook. After dinner we walked for an hour in the woods, the silver moon gleaming through the branches. R. a charming companion. Before going to bed, he showed me a truly deep and beautiful page in one of Newman's Sermons. When I can get the proper volume, I shall like to transcribe it. [Would that he had transcribed it in this book!] Among other things, he wondered how it was that members of Parliament came to see me so much, and to talk so freely to me. "They never come to me," he said. *J. M.* "You're too big a man for one thing, and for another you are uncertain — not always to be found. I am always there, you see." *R.* "Oh, that's not it. When I was in every morning at Lansdowne House, 't was just the same. No, you are sympathetic." This comparison paid me an undeserved compliment, for nobody surpassed him in that inner humanity which is the root of good manners and good feeling and other things lying at the core of character.

A triple alliance in Parliament, a sermon of Newman's, perfect service and the glamour of moonlight, sympathy and the core of character — it was of such strands as these that the cord of politics and society was twisted; and all the while he who helps in the spinning is standing with the fatal shears ready, if he may, to cut the thin-spun thread. Liberalism may bring with it the promise of many blessings to mankind, it may even be preparing the world for a society intrinsically finer than the old — I do not know — but for the privileged graces of aristocracy it certainly has little heed; and Morley was the very type of the Liberal who relishes all the pleasures of privilege while advocating every measure of reform which would make them no longer possible. It is of the essence of his whole life that, having at the close of his active career accepted, or rather chosen for himself, a seat in the House of Lords, he immediately set himself to carry through a bill which should deprive that body of its power and prerogative. Say what one will and making allow-

ance for any necessity of the move, there is a
taint of ingratitude, of unconscious duplicity one
might say, in such a procedure. There is this
paradox, if you will call it so, in Morley's attitude
towards society, comparable to that of his attitude towards Oxford.

Perhaps thoughtlessness is a more appropriate
word than ingratitude, unless, indeed, the two
epithets come in the end to the same thing. The
fact is that Morley, save in matters of taste, is
not a man of originality, nor even of steady reflection; he never quite came to terms with himself in regard to the ideas which he took over
from his teachers. In religion and politics he was
a professed follower of John Stuart Mill, a utilitarian agnostic and Liberal; yet one cannot read
together the biographical works of Mill and the
Recollections of Morley without feeling the profound difference between the mind of the master,
who, to some degree at least, felt the deeper com-
plexities of life beneath the system he was creating, and the mind of the pupil, who took the
system as a finished formula and carried it on
ruthlessly. Read Morley's three essays on Mill.
There is something almost amusing in the change
of tone from the first two, in which he celebrates
his master as "one of those high and most
worthy spirits" who never falter or compromise
in their pursuit of pure truth, to the third essay,
written as a reply to Mill's posthumous volume

on religion. Lord Morley tells us in his *Recollections* with what consternation he learned that the thinker and complete agnostic of his reverence had fallen back at the last upon the belief, shadowy indeed yet almost orthodox, in a wise and beneficent Creator and upon the hope of immortality. Let us admit a strain of inconsistency in Mill's mental make-up. I have said elsewhere that he is the example *par excellence* of a philosopher who combines the most lucid powers of exposition with an incapacity of clear thinking, and I believe this could be demonstrated not only from the incompatibility between his earlier positivism and his later sentimentalism (or intuition, if you prefer), but from his position at any given moment of his life. Yet, after all, if inconsistency must be reckoned lower than the consistency of clear insight, it still has its virtue when compared with a consistency bought at the price of spiritual blindness. And in Mill the confession that seemed to his disciple only a weak retraction was really the final utterance of a deep uneasiness with his own rational theories, which at a moment in his youth had thrown him into a mood of dark despair like Coleridge's *Dejection*, and which, though generally concealed, continued always to lie beneath his heart. There were in Mill stirrings of doubt, of wise scepticism, which the Oxford scholar, in his consistent hostility to the spirit of Oxford, never fathomed.

His only substitute for these would appear to be the art of commenting prettily on the universality of death.

Nor does Morley give any sign that he ever in his active years felt Mill's hesitations in regard to the ulterior consequences of social reform. There is a problem that has lain heavily upon the conscience of the more philosophic Radicals, a problem that Mill faced honestly in his treatise on *Liberty* — the natural antagonism between the equality to which progress looks as its practical end and that freedom of the individual the benefit and necessity of which might seem to be recognized in the very name of Liberalism. Were it not for a habit of obstinate forgetfulness in human nature we should think it needless to recall the great passages wherein Morley's acknowledged teacher dilates on "the tyranny of opinion" almost inevitable in a State governed by the immediate will of the majority — a tyranny more far-reaching in its grasp than the arbitrary despotism of any single man or group of men. And Mill, the progressive Radical, was not blind to the peculiar tendency of this tyranny to produce a condition of dead mediocrity. "All the political changes of the age," he declares, "promote it [this level of mediocrity], since they all tend to raise the low and to lower the high. Every extension of education promotes it, because education brings people under common in-

fluences, and gives them access to the general
stock of facts and sentiments. Improvement in
the means of communication promotes it, by
bringing the inhabitants of distant places into
personal contact, and keeping up a rapid flow of
changes of residence between one place and another. The increase of commerce and manufac-
tures promotes it, by diffusing more widely the
advantages of easy circumstances, and opening
all objects of ambition, even the highest, to general competition, whereby the desire of rising
becomes no longer the character of a particular
class, but of all classes. A more powerful agency
than even all these, in bringing about a general
similarity among mankind, is the complete estab-
lishment, in this and other free countries, of the
ascendency of public opinion in the State. As the
various social eminences which enabled persons
entrenched on them to disregard the opinion of
the multitude gradually become leveled; as the
very idea of resisting the will of the public, when
it is positively known that they have a will, dis-
appears more and more from the minds of practical politicians; there ceases to be any social
support for non-conformity — any substantive
power in society, which, itself opposed to the
ascendency of numbers, is interested in taking
under its protection opinions and tendencies at
variance with those of the public."

And so we have, as Mill would say, this clamorous paradox: an equalitarian Liberalism is based on and justified by the doctrine of progress, yet by its own weight tends to depress that variety of situations and that liberty of the individual which are the efficient causes of progress. Mill's own solution of this difficulty depends on the feasibility of training the better endowed few to a consciousness of the obligations of self-development and public leadership, and on faith in the natural instinct of the masses of mankind to follow a true guide; he would give to education the place in society which Burke gave to prerogative. But I do not raise these perplexing questions for the sake of criticising Liberalism or for the purpose of considering plausible remedies. My aim is entirely the more modest one of pointing to a certain thoughtlessness, a certain unheeding straightforwardness, in the mind of a man like Morley who, while enjoying and frankly eulogizing the distinctions of a society based on the higher individualism, yet never hesitated in carrying through measures which, as he himself knew, were laying the axe at the roots of such a society. Though he knew this, you will find, at least within the compass of the *Recollections*, no regret for the ambiguity of his position, no anxious self-questioning such as troubled Mill.

This difference between Mill and Morley is significant of much, but we are brought even closer, I think, to the heart of Morley's Liberalism by considering his relation to two earlier writers — Burke and Rousseau. Now if there be two names in the history of sociology more antipodal to each other than these, I do not know them; and it is extraordinary, to say the least, that throughout his life Morley has professed himself an admirer and, to a certain extent, a follower of both of these men. This is verily a compromise worthy of a new chapter in his treatise on that subject, a compromise indicative of some dulness of the mind to the law of mutual exclusions, possible only to one who has never really assimilated what is essential to one or both of the terms included. As for Burke, Morley's attitude towards that enemy of destructive innovation is more than extraordinary. One of his earliest ventures in literature was an essay, in large measure eulogistic, on the author of the *Reflections on the French Revolution*, and in 1907 Burke is still, he assures a correspondent, "a high idol of mine." That is consistent enough, but the remarkable thing is the grounds of this continued admiration. More than once in the *Recollections* he avows that what he learnt from Burke was the "practical principles in the strategy and tactics of public life," and for this lesson he accepts Macaulay's estimation of Burke as "the greatest man since Milton." Such praise for such a benefit is rather startling, but surprise turns to amazement when we find that this teacher of practical politics was, according to the statement of Lord Lansdowne quoted with approval in Morley's life of Burke, "so violent, so overbearing, so arrogant, so intractable, that to have got on with him in a cabinet would have been utterly and absolutely impossible." And if Morley acquired from Burke a virtue — for of practical politics of the more honourable sort Morley was a past master — of which Burke himself was the doubtful possessor, he quite failed, on the other hand, to take from him the one quality of imaginative perception which gives meaning to the whole of Burke's career. Of this quality, to be sure, Morley's critical intelligence was fully aware when he wrote his monograph. He saw its positive aspect: Burke, he says, "was using no idle epithet, when he described the disposition of a stupendous wisdom, 'moulding together the great mysterious incorporation of the human race.'" And he saw also its negative aspect, the inhibition exercised by the higher centripetal imagination upon the egotistic expansiveness of the individual. This, he avers, was with Burke "the cardinal truth for men, namely, that if you encourage every individual to let the imagination loose upon all subjects, without any restraint from a sense of his own weakness, and his subordinate rank in the long scheme of things, then there is nothing of all that the opinion of ages has agreed to regard as excellent and venerable, which would not be exposed to destruction at the hands of rationalistic criticism." The strange thing is that one who could analyse Burke's political creed so fairly and express it so sympathetically should persistently profess himself a follower of Burke for qualities which Burke possessed superficially, if he possessed them at all. The simple fact is, I suspect, that Morley appreciates Burke by the contact of what may be called a purely literary imagination, and by a certain sympathy of character, whereas in the higher imagination as an actual controlling element of statesmanship, or in that deeper wisdom of the human heart which goes with it, he is profoundly deficient. So it is I explain to myself his almost callous indifference, so far as the records show, to the destructive hazard in a rationalistic programme, which even a Mill could perceive.

In the case of the other great leader to whom Morley remains addicted throughout life, the procedure is of a reverse order. With Burke our statesman feels himself in sympathy, whatever he may say of Parliamentary strategy, chiefly by reason of the British tradition of sturdy character, while he rejects the principle upon which that character is really based. To Rousseau he is drawn in a contrary manner. Here it is the central impulse of the heart, the generating principle of conduct, that holds his loyalty. Early in the

Recollections he quotes, as justifying his own addiction to Rousseau, a passage from a letter of George Eliot, that throws a flood of light on the nature of his Liberalism. "I wish you to understand," the novelist had written, "that the writers who have most profoundly interested me — who have rolled away the waters from their bed, raised new mountains and spread delicious valleys for me — are not in the least oracles to me. It is just possible that I may not embrace one of their opinions — that I may wish my life to be shaped quite differently from theirs. For instance it would signify nothing to me if a very wise person were to stun me with proofs that Rousseau's views of life, religion, and government are miserably erroneous. . . . I might admit all this, and it would be not the less true that Rousseau's genius has sent that electric thrill through my intellectual and moral frame which has awakened me to new perceptions — which has made man and nature a world of freer thought and feeling to me; and this not by teaching me any new belief."

Now a plain man might be inclined to ask by what right a practical statesman, however it may be with a maker of fiction, dare avow his adherence to a philosopher who kindles a relentless flame of passion, yet whose "views of life, religion, and government are miserably erroneous." It might be in order to observe that this reckless surrender to emotion, without conscientious scruples for the direction the emotion was taking, has been one of the causes which have brought the world to its present dolorous pass. But at bottom Morley has taken from Rousseau something more than the mere shock of feeling. As one may learn from many passages of the *Recollections*, there are involved with this emotionalism two leading ideas, or views of life, distinct in expression, though springing from the same head. One of these is what he calls "Rousseau's resplendent commonplace," and is directly political: "'T is the people that compose the human race; what is not people is so small a concern that it is not worth the trouble of counting." The other idea is rather the philosophical, or psychological, basis of Rousseauism. It is what Morley in various places upholds as the law of "bold free expansion," "the gospel of free intellectual and social expansion"; it is the "belief in Progress" as the mechanical result of this expansive instinct, which he insistently preaches as a substitute for the belief in God and providence. It might be remarked in passing that these two Rousseauistic ideas are in violent opposition to the doctrine of Morley's other acknowledged master. To conceive society as composed of the people alone (the masses, that is, as contrasted with the privileged classes) is certainly, whatever else may be said of it, to deny any meaning to Burke's notion of the hierarchy of orders forming together "the great mysterious incorporation of the human race"; it is even to forget the reservations of leadership demanded by so complete a Liberal as Mill. And, again, to trust for progress to an instinctive desire of expansion in human nature is certainly to encourage that letting loose of the individual imagination, without any restraint from the sense of a man's own weakness, about which Burke would throw the bulwark of the restrictive social imagination.

But that is by the way. The striking fact is that no one could be more sensitive than Morley to the actual outcome of these principles in character, yet that he should so entirely overlook the nexus of cause and effect. Of Rousseau's personal weaknesses he was an unsparing critic; he has written of them in the spirit of Burke and of an English gentleman. Theoretically, too, he knows that such fine emotional words as "truth, right, and general good," if allowed to usurp the place of plain thinking, may be nothing more than a cloak for factious malignity; he can praise Bishop Butler for "the solid distinction of never shutting his eyes to dark facts in human life and history." Yet one might suppose, for anything said in the *Recollections*, that there is no connection between Rousseau's theory of natural goodness and that lack of personal reticence in speech and conduct which make his character so repul-

sive. And in his political course, again as reflected in the *Recollections*, Morley is content to
reiterate his confidence in the British workman
as a being whose desires will instinctively limit
themselves without any outer control, as if here
the "dark facts" of selfishness did not exist.
"My faith," he writes in a letter after the Kai-
ser's visit to London, "in the political prudence
of our democracy is unshaken, and I don't wonder that the German Emperor should have
wished that his men of that kidney were half as
sensible." It is probable that Lord Morley, in
his present retirement, has changed his opinion
somewhat in respect to William, and does not
now, as he did in 1907, when cajoled by that
Monarch's table talk, regard the Imperial Government as solely intent on preserving "a little
decent calm all over Europe." One wonders
whether he has seen a light also in respect to the
possible greed of a class of men who find the way
open to grasp at unlimited political power. Will
it occur to him that in the one case as in the
other, in the Pan-Germanism of Berlin as in the
programme of British Radicalism, there is at
work the same law of untrammelled expansiveness, and that there may be some peril in following the electric thrill of freer feeling as a force
beautiful and ennobling in itself, whatever may
be the accompanying views of life, religion, and
government? Long ago the first Marquess of

Halifax, who had learnt much in the hard school of revolution, discovered that "the greatest part of the business of the world is the effect of not thinking." How far is the business of the world to-day the result of feeling without thinking?

I must say again, and emphatically, that I am not writing a political treatise, nor am I attempting to weigh the good and evil of Radicalism in general. My task is the humbler one of trying to analyse the character of a particular Radical. Here before us lies his autobiography: it is a life replete with charm, most of what was best in the literature of the day is reflected in it, and much of the culture of antiquity; the traditional graces of society give it lustre, and it is actuated by a steady and unselfish purpose; yet what is the conclusion? At the end of the record, as a kind of epilogue, the statesman who had played a part in the social changes of an epoch, describes a walk in a Surrey upland with little Eileen, a four-footed favourite, and these are the closing words:

A painful interrogatory, I must confess, emerges. Has not your school — the Darwins, Spencers, Renans, and the rest — held the civilized world, both old and new alike, European and transatlantic, in the hollow of their hand for two long generations past? Is it quite clear that their influence has been so much more potent than the gospel of the various churches? *Circumspice.* Is not diplomacy, unkindly called by Voltaire the field of lies, as able as it ever was to dupe governments and governed by grand abstract catchwords veiling obscure and inexplicable purposes, and turning the whole world over with blood and tears to a strange Witches' Sabbath? These were queries of pith and moment indeed, but for something better weighed and more deliberative than an autumn reverie.

Now and then I paused as I sauntered slow over the fading heather. My little humble friend squat on her haunches, looking wistfully up, eager to resume her endless hunt after she knows not what, just like the chartered metaphysicians. So to my home in the falling daylight.

I am not wrong, I think, in being disconcerted by such a conclusion to such a record. Is all our intelligence and all our aspiration after the truth no more than the wistful and aimless searching of a dog? I believe that no man is justified in laying his hand on the complicated fabric of society until he has a surer sense of direction than this; and I am tempted to ask whether the Witches' Sabbath into which we had reeled (this was the time of the war) may not have been the natural goal of a world divided between those who follow the instinct of expansion without feeling, and those who follow the same instinct without thinking. If British statesmen like Lord Morley and Sir Edward Grey and British scholars like Gilbert Murray had not been so steeped in the illusion of human righteousness as to discredit the possibility of war, would the war have occurred? It may be unfair to drag in these stupendous issues when criticising the work of one who was, after all, a

minor figure in the politics of the day; but Lord
Morley is a type. And waiving these considerations, there is still the uncomfortable fact that
Lord Morley seems never to have reflected seriously — never, at least, until too late — on the
ambiguous position of a statesman who accepted
the ungrudged gifts of a culture and a society
which all the while he was deliberately under-
mining. Such action bears at least the semblance
of ingratitude. And if it is the ingratitude born
of magnanimous sympathy for the less fortunate,
one must still ask whether sympathy, unbal-
anced by clear understanding of human nature
and uncontrolled by the larger imagination, may
not be found in the end on the side of the destructive rather than the constructive forces of
civilization. These disturbing doubts, despite
our admiration for Lord Morley, will arise in regard to the special form of utilitarian Liberalism
which he took from Mill, without Mill's anxiety;
they bring to mind the strong words of Leopardi:

> Stolta, che l'util chiede,
> E inutile la vita
> Quindi più sempre divenir non vede.[1]

---

[1] *Il Pensiero Dominante:* "Blind! that demands the useful, and sees not that ever thence life becomes more useless."

ECONOMIC IDEALS

ECONOMIC IDEALS

ON the slip-cover of Mr. Ernest Poole's story of
The Harbour, which I have read rather belatedly,
the publishers have printed this legend: "The
central character is a young man who, through
his intimate contact with people and particularly through his study of humanity as it ebbs
and flows in the great harbour, comes finally to
see the inner meaning of things." And we learn
that the book is regarded by one at least of our
great newspapers as "the best American novel
that has appeared in many a long day." Of the
literary merit of Mr Poole's work I am not concerned to speak. As a mere piece of fiction it will
be outbid by some noisier competitor to-morrow,
if it is not already forgotten; but as an honest
and forcible presentation of a vital problem it has
more than passing interest. Not that the author
has brought any new thoughts to bear on the
vexing questions he propounds, or has reached to
"the inner meaning of things." It would be truer
to say that he has not thought at all; and indeed
the value of his book lies in the clarity with which
the current ideas and emotions of the hour find
expression in his pages, without taking any colour
from their passage through his mind or suffering
any distortion from an original imagination.

The plot of the story may be recalled. A young man, who develops into a writer, has been brought up in peculiarly intimate relations with the shipping of New York Harbour, and a good deal of the book is given up to vivid pictures of the multiform life about the shores of the North and East Rivers. At college — Princetonians have not been slow to recognize their alma mater in the unflattering scenes — he discovers the emptiness and dull conventionality of academic tradition; one can scarcely say academic education, for apparently he learns nothing in chapel or lecture room. But here he becomes acquainted with a rebellious youth from the Middle West, a certain Joe Kramer, who distinguishes himself by doing a little independent thinking, as his creator understands thinking, and who is destined later on to exert a decisive influence on the hero. "Do you know who's to blame for this stuff?" queries our indignant young philosopher. "It's not the profs, I've nothing against them, all they need is to be kicked out. No. It's us, because we stand for their line of drule. If we got right up on our honkeys and howled, all of us, for a real education, we'd get it by next Saturday night. But we don't care a damn" — an observation which is not without a measure of truth. One is not surprised to learn that Joe had as little reverence for the tradition of literature as for its teachers: "This darned library shut its

doors," he would growl to himself, "just as the
real dope was coming along. But there's been
such a flood of it ever since that some leaked in in
spite of 'em."

Owing to his good fortune in meeting Joe, our
hero came out of college with some "enlight-
enment" despite his professors. But at first,
through his love for a girl he had known as a
child, and now sees again in the plenitude of
her charms, he is thrown much with an engineer
named Dillon, her father, a dreamer absorbed in
schemes for making New York the great organ-
ized centre of the world's trade. The quiet assurance of the man captivates him, and he is carried
away by the stupendous vision of a society regen-
erated and controlled by the hand of scientific
efficiency working in harmony with the beneficent
powers of capital. With a reminiscence, one imagines, of the Temptation in the Wilderness, the
author conveys us, with his hero, into Dillon's
offices high up in the tower of the Woolworth
Building, from whence we look down upon the
panorama of the city and the bay, as upon the
kingdoms of the world, lying now in haphazard
confusion as things have grown up by chance.
And then the engineer displays his charts of the
harbour as it is to be, with its continuous docks
and vast organization of machinery. Along the
heavy roofs of steel are drawn wide ocean boule-
vards, with trees and shrubs and flowers to shut

out the clamorous business below; and the port itself is no longer a mere body of water, but has beneath it a whole region of tunnels, through which is flowing the endless traffic, unseen and unheard. All this the city was to build, and as landlord was to invite the shipping and railway lords and the manufacturers to come in and "get together," and work with one another and the city in the mighty plan. "That's what we mean nowadays by a port," explains the deviser of the great project, "a complicated industrial organ, the heart of a country's circulation, pumping in and out its millions of tons of traffic as quickly and cheaply as possible. That's efficiency, scientific management, or just plain engineering, whatever you want to call it. But it's got to be done for us all in a plan, instead of each for himself in a blind struggling chaos." Later, as a writer of "glory stories," the inquisitive young man gains the intimacy of the financial magnate who, from his office in Wall Street, is controlling all these new forces of reconstruction. And as the money-lord talks, and lays bare the tremendous schemes of promotion that find their centre there in those quiet rooms, our hero beholds again the vision he had beheld in the tower; he feels the dazzling future, as it were rushing upon the world, a future of plenty and power, governed by the keen minds and wide outlook of the strong men at the top.

Then comes what a Greek tragedian would call the *peripeteia*. Suddenly Joe Kramer reappears upon the scene, and the supposedly blind unconscious instruments of the vast reconstruction, the labourers who supplied the physical energy for the moving traffic of the harbour, are united in a strike against their masters — a strike which in the eyes of their leaders is merely the beginning of a universal revolt against an age-long condition of servitude. At first our hero is on the side of the employers. "What's your main idea," he exclaims to Joe, "in stirring up millions of ignorant men? Your stokers and dock labourers are about as fit to build up a new world as they are to build a Brooklyn Bridge. Can't you see you're all just floundering in a perfect swamp of ignorance?" But he is carried by Joe down into the stoke-hole of a vessel and made to see the terrible existence (in itself overdrawn, if this were a question of truth) of the slaves to the demon of fire and to the god of efficiency; he is admitted to meetings of the strikers in which the feeling of participation in a common cause breaks down the barriers between workers from every part of the globe. Gradually he is transformed by a clearer perception of what it all means. These tragic people gripped him hard. The crippled dockers in their homes — with their women and children, their agony, and the fear of starvation looming up before them — brought a tightening at his throat. But it was not only sympathy that moved him; doubts of his former creed were awakened within him, and admiration for the power of this new ideal that was teaching multitudes of men to act as if impelled by a single purpose. Far to the south, high over all the squalid tenement dwellings, rose that tower of lights he had known so well, the airy palace where Dillon had dreamed and planned his clean vigorous world. He saw its lights gleaming above the city as though nothing was happening here on the water front. He thought of the men about him. How crassly ignorant they seemed. And yet in a few brief hours they had paralyzed all that the tower had planned, reduced it all to silence, nothing. Could it be, he asked himself, that such upheavals as these meant an end to the rule of the world from above, by the keen minds at the top? Was that great idol which he had worshipped for so many years, that last of his gods, Efficiency, beginning to rock a little now upon its deep foundations?

Outwardly the strike fails, under the combined conspiracy of capital, the press, and the government; but to our hero it is no failure, rather it is the mere skirmishing preparatory to the great battle that is to alter the whole course of civilization. Nor is it a question of labour only, a temporary dispute over dollars and cents; it is the fermentation of a new philosophy that is to supplant all the old beliefs — a philosophy of sheer change, involving a perfect trust in the undirected will of the universe, whether manifesting itself in the unreasoned instincts of mankind or in the dumb forces of inanimate nature, to move ever of its own accord on and on to better destinies. "I believe," says an English novelist to our hero one day, putting into words what has long been gathering in his mind — "I believe the age we live in is changing so much faster than any age before it, that a man if he's to be vital at all must give up the idea of any fixed creed — in his office, his church, or his home — that if he does not he will only wear himself out butting his indignant head against what is stronger and probably better than he. But if he does, if he holds himself open to change and knows that change is his very life, then he can get a serenity which is as much better than that of the monk as living is better than dying." Thus the idol of Efficiency, whose devotees dreamed of a world managed and made beautiful by the hands of science and money, is shattered before his eyes, while in its place rises the image of the People, as themselves, moving by the blind centripetal force of sympathy and by obedience to their changing instincts, securely onward to happiness and peace. As the publishers of his history proclaim, somewhat grandiosely, he is brought to know "the inner meaning of things."

No one, we think, will read this book without feeling that it is a faithful echo of the currents of thought sweeping over a large portion of the world. Mr. Poole has spoken the truth as the majority of his contemporaries see it, but it is still possible to ask whether he has spoken the whole truth, even the truth as it is. What if there is a terrible omission in our perception of the facts of life as he gives it back to us in this allegory? What if the fluctuation of our minds between the ideals of scientific control and socialistic combination should prove to be a sign that we have lost the clear steady conception of anything really worth while to be gained by controlling or combining? Is there no conceivable excellence of the soul itself but efficiency on the one side, with the confidence in progress wrung from the increasing mastery of material forces, or, on the other side, sympathy with the instinctive thrust of masses of men pressing for their close-seen advantage? Or, even granting the possibility, unrecognized by Mr. Poole, of reconciling the control from above of scientific knowledge with the clamour from below of immediate wants, where is the promise of happiness in such a world unless something else is added?

This is just what strikes us in the philosophy of Mr. Poole's book, what indeed sends us with a feeling of contraction and depression from almost all the sociological books we read, whether

they take the form of fiction or "science" —
this naïve ignorance of individual life as a thing
possibly valuable in itself and worthy of cultivation. The complete lack of any such idea is
apparently unconscious, but the effect is felt.
Through all the clamour for life, pure life, liberated from the mouldy grip of antiquity, if you
listen attentively you will hear the troubled, be-
wildered voice of men who, like gearless ships,
are desperately signalling for aid. You need not
be deceived; this joy which is promised to men if
they will abandon their allegiance to any fixed
law, is a pure illusion.

Suppose we took the crude antithesis presented to us. Is it true that he who throws himself unreservedly open to the stream of change
will attain to a serenity which is as much better
than that of the monk, as living is better than
dying? History would scarcely admit it. I suspect that a Saint Bernard, in the seclusion of his
convent at Clairvaux after one of his expeditions
into the world, won from his absorbed contemplation of a God who knows no shadow of turning, a peace and a strength of which there is no
intimation in the fretful literature of change. It
was not the love of nature as we understand it
which caused him to say to his friends, in his
gracious manner of jesting, that his wisdom
came less from books than from meditation in
the woods and fields; it was rather his conviction

that power is gained in the silences of the soul.
And he was a powerful man. From his cell he
spoke words that shook the governments of the
world; there has probably never been a man who
exercised more practical authority over his contemporaries than this monk whose life was but
a dying.

But this criticism is only in the interest of his-
toric truth, and has slight bearing on the problems of the present. We certainly are not pleading now for the monkish ideal of life. The question comes closer to us when we apply the test to
those men who, to Joe Kramer and his like, are
the drones of our own civilization. Now, in considering Mr. Poole's diatribe against the universities, we ought to remember that, with his
narrowly and typically contemporaneous view,
he is looking at these institutions strictly as they
are at the moment. We must recollect the degree
to which the academic aim has been modified
under pressure from without, and how largely
instruction has become scientific and economic,
dominated by the future interest of the student
in material efficiency and social reform. The
keynote of education is given by that maleficent
phrase of ex-President Eliot: *For power and service*. One need only examine the statistics of
courses elected, or hear the talk and public dis-
sertations of undergraduates, to learn how prev-
alent is this ideal. At the same time the college

has retained a certain tincture of tradition, and still professes, however meekly, to impart instruction in the humanities. It has so far lagged behind in the march of progress that it has become neither unrepentantly an engineering school, nor frankly an experimental station for applied sociology, nor yet exclusively a combination of these two. A certain amount of "drule" is still thrust down the throat of recalcitrant youth in the form of "cultural" and useless learning.

Now what is the consequence of this indolent compromise? The instructors for the most part feel themselves to be lecturing, so to speak, *in vacuo*. "The faculty, as a whole," says Mr. Poole's honest young collegian, "appeared to me no less fatigued; most of them lectured as though getting tired, the others as though tired out." Alas, these "poor dry devils" were not so much tired as baffled. Those who were carrying large classes through the acceptable courses in science and sociology might be jaunty and, in the presence of their less favoured colleagues, a trifle supercilious; but most of them probably felt the unreality of their work in the class-room, in comparison with the vitality of similar interests in the practical world. As for the others, those who were clinging to the shreds of the humanities left them, they no doubt talked with the desperation of men beaten in the race, and, like as not, could give no articulate reason why they should not be beaten. Too often, the college professor is a man who has been deprived of the opportunity of dulling consciousness *in dem Strom der Welt*, and has gained in return no strong conviction of the privilege of scholarship in itself and for its rewards to the scholar himself.

A glance at the academic literature of the past hundred years would show a remarkable change in this respect. In the early part of the nineteenth century an earnest man who gained a fellowship at Oxford or Cambridge was congratulated as if one of the prizes of life had fallen to him. Now, take up any book of the present day, and if it touches on the universities, it will probably affect the mocking tone of *The Harbour*, or, with more dignity, will smile away the scholar's pretensions to serious consideration, in the manner of Hugh Walpole in *The Prelude to Adventure*. The Englishman's gentle irony is really worthy of quotation at some length:

There are those who adopt Cambridge as their abiding home, and it is for these that real life is impossible. Beneath these gray walls as the years pass slowly the illusions grow. Closer and closer creep the walls of experience, softer and thicker are the garments worn to keep out the cold, gentler and gentler are the speculations born of a good old Port and a knowledge of the Greek language. About the High Tables voices softly dispute the turning of a phrase, eyes mildly salute the careful dishes of a wisely chosen cook, gentle patronage

is bestowed upon the wild ruffian of the outer world.
Many bells ring, many fires are burning, many lamps are
lit, many leaves of many books are turned — busily,
busily hands are raising walls of self-defence; the world
at first regretted, then patronized, is now forgotten...
hush, he sleeps, his feet in slippers, his head upon the
softest cushion, his hand still covering the broad page
of his dictionary.... Nothing, not birth nor love, nor
death must disturb his repose.

That is the English university from the outside, just as Mr. Poole gave an American college
from the outside, but the voice of the scholar
from within is not so very different. I was struck
the other day by a passage in the catalogue of
Blackwell, the Oxford book-seller, copied from
L. R. Farnell's obituary of the late Ingram By-
water. After drawing a portrait of the learned
Aristotelian as a "perfect example of the votary
of the life intellectual," a man of noble presence
and distinguished manners, fond of his peers and
capable of shining in such society, Mr. Farnell
concludes thus: "Such a life and such a type may
not be thought to be the highest; but if Acade-
mies are still to continue and to flourish, we must
hope that such types will continue to be produced and to be valued; and that life is to be
counted happy which pursues a spiritual ideal
and preserves it undimmed to the end." Hand-
some words you will say. They are; but why this
deprecatory comparison with a career in the
world? why this deference to opinion? It is,

I fear, because the Oxford don, like the rest of us, has grown a little doubtful of the value of life itself as it may be developed in the privileged leisure of learning. We are half apologetic for the man who, primarily for himself and secondarily for others, esteems it a thing worth while to raise his thoughts into communion with the great minds of the past, and honours the labour of the spirit so to purify itself that it may be at home in the world of Ideas. Only those scholars are quite free of this kind of distrust who, as practical scientists or sociologists, turn the college into a laboratory for the mill or the legislature. The much decried vanity of the *vita umbratilis* is in fact only one phase of the general doubt of any positive value in life, with the added disadvantage that he who lives in the shadow of intellectual studies is deprived of the narcotic of unreflective action. If the emptiness is clearer to the college man than to his brother in the world, it is because, after all, he still has some opportunity for reflection, and retains a vestige of the habit of self-examination.

Without subscribing to the Nietzschean remedies, one may point to the accuracy with which Nietzsche has touched the two sources underlying this state of "nihilism," as he names it. "A 'scientific' interpretation of the world as you understand it," he says, "might consequently still be one of the stupidest, that is to say, the most destitute of significance, of all possible world interpretations.... An essentially mechanical world would be an essentially meaningless world." The corollary to this saying is headed, *The Moral Fashion of a Commercial Community*, and runs thus:

Behind the principle of the present moral fashion — "Moral actions are actions performed out of sympathy for others" — I see the social instinct of fear, which thus assumes an intellectual disguise.... How little joy must men now have in themselves when such a tyranny of fear prescribes their supreme moral law.

These are the two bases of the critical phase — which is also the sound phase — of Nietzsche's philosophy, and no one, I think, will fail to be struck by their correspondence with the two aspects of life as presented in *The Harbour*. As we contemplate the world converted into a huge machine and managed by engineers, we gradually grow aware of its lack of meaning, of its emptiness of human value; the soul is stifled in this glorification of mechanical efficiency. And then we begin to feel the weakness of such a creed when confronted by the real problems of life; we discover its inability to impose any restraint on the passions of men, or to supply any government which can appeal to the loyalty of the spirit. And seeing these things we understand the fear that is gnawing at the vitals of society. If you do not at first see how this social instinct of fear may enter into the scientific interpretation of the world, consider Mr. Poole's parting retort upon the governments which for the time suppressed his revolutionary friends:

Your civilization is crashing down. For a hundred years, in all our strikes and risings, you preached against our violence — you talked of your law and order, your clear deliberate thinking. In you lay the hope of the world, you said. You were Civilization. You were Mind and Science, in you was all Efficiency, in you was Art, Religion; and you kept the Public Peace. But now you have broken all your vows. The world's treasures of Art are as safe with you as they were in the Dark Ages. Your Prince of Peace you have trampled down. And all your Science you have turned to the efficient slaughter of men. In a week of your boasted calmness you have plunged the world into a violence beside which all the bloodshed in our strikes and revolutions seems like a pool beside the sea. And so you have failed, you powers above, blindly and stupidly you have failed. For you have let loose a violence where you are weak and we are strong. We are these armies that you have called out.

There you have it. You cannot escape it. Germany has been the most scientifically efficient country of the world; it has approached most nearly to the ideal of the Harbour as this was seen in the dreams of a Dillon; and Germany has not only been unable to prevent the catastrophe of the most hideous war in history, but has been the prime cause of that war. Scientific evolution without a corresponding moral evolution, scientific evolution absorbing the thoughts of men to the exclusion of other considerations, has not brought greater control of the savage passions of men, but has simply created more efficient instruments for the use of those passions. We pretend, of course, to be shocked by this uprush of barbarism through our civilization, but in reality we are not much surprised. Deep down in our consciousness all the while we have known the fear of this amid all our boasted optimism. Fear — there has been, and is, a great fear at the heart of the world. Among the proletariat it is the fear, not wholly unjustified, of being exploited as mere inhuman cogs in a machine; for what, they have asked themselves, has scientific evolution to do with the heart and spirit or with human hopes and joys and regrets? And so the proletariat has banded itself together as a fighting army against its exploiters. Mr. Poole exalts this uniting bond as sympathy, but it is sympathy which derives its holding power from a community of fear and hatred, and is therefore purely destructive in its nature. It may ruin society; it can build up nothing. On the other side, among the intelligent and successful, this fear has taken the form of humanitarian repentance; it has reared a morality of sympathy and sops in place of obligation and command. Humanitarianism, as Nietzsche showed, is merely an intellectual disguise for the social instinct of fear; the attempt to keep men in subordination by kind words. There is no doubt of the fact. This instinctive fear has been troubling the organizers and masters of society for many years. They have betrayed its presence by their charities, by their hatreds, their abstinences, their restless pursuit of amusement. Beneath their bravado they have had an uneasy consciousness that not all was well with their programme of scientific efficiency, and that some day the whole complicated fabric might come toppling down about their ears; and now the hideous confusion of war has risen like a spectre to leave them with no defence against the questioning of a society to which they had made themselves responsible.[1]

Those who regard the present war as essentially social in its character are right. It is, at bottom, not so much a conflict of governments as the outburst of passions which have long been seething in the breast of mankind, the outburst of fear most of all, the fear of man for man. And that fear we shall not eliminate by more scientific efficiency; we shall not eliminate it by any means, but we may possibly change its direction and its object.

Fear, I suspect, has always been a stronger motive in human conduct than we like to admit,

---

[1] Mr. Poole's book was published and this essay was written during the war. It has not seemed worth while to change the tenses of my verbs.

however the world at large may seem to pursue
its even and stolid course. We live by allowance,
so to speak, and have no security in our tenure.
Everywhere about us are unseen forces which, at
a moment and without warning, may leap upon
us out of the darkness. A little chance, and our
means of support may be rent away from us; an
infinitesimal organism floating in the air we
breathe may suddenly turn our vital powers into
torment; at the best we are but debtors to the
grave. For two thousand years each generation of
mankind has been repeating to itself the Virgilian
felicitation of the rare man who has put under
his feet all the fears of life and inexorable fate.

Among the Greeks and Romans this lubricity
of fortune was symbolized in the so-called envy
of the gods; with the Christians it was transformed into the jealousy of the Lord. But it
corresponded with the same feeling in either
case, the haunting suspicion that there is somewhere a Power jealous of man's autonomy, and
certain, though by methods often strangely incomprehensible, to take vengeance upon arrogant self-assertion or overweening confidence in
the favour of fortune. Man cannot imagine himself in a world of immoral chance or unmeaning
change; if he reflects at all he is driven to translate the devious work of fate into a law of retribu-
tive justice. The spectre is of a Power that cannot be escaped. Man has fled —

Adown Titanic glooms of chasmèd fears,
　From those strong Feet that followed, followed after.
　　But with unhurrying chase,
　　And unperturbèd pace,
　Deliberate speed, majestic instancy,
　　They beat — and a Voice beat
　　More instant than the Feet —
　"All things betray thee, who betrayest Me."

Is not our position to-day something like that?
The wrath of a celestial Judge we may have reasoned or laughed away, but it does not follow
that we have argued ourselves out of the ancient
dread; we have merely brought down fear from
heaven to earth, giving to sociology what we
have taken from religion. Having made the
People our judge, we have attempted to appease
our deity by a service of sympathy, only to discover that we have put into its hands an instrument of revenge. Sympathy has been grasped by
the People as a law of combination for themselves and in defiance of their rulers. The result
is not harmony, but a division of society such as
we see it portrayed in *The Harbour*.

And so, if fear is an inevitable factor of human
conduct, it is reasonable to ask whether the old
religious dread may not be a sounder starting-
point than social sympathy, whether there may
not be some truth in the discarded saying that
the beginning of wisdom is to fear God and keep
his commandments; or, at least, whether we

should not be advised to acknowledge once more the existence of a Nemesis, or power that makes for righteousness, or whatever we may choose to call the law that speaks to the heart of a man and holds him individually responsible for his acts. Possibly, if we had listened less to the voice of society, and more to the voice of duty commanding us to make ourselves right with our own higher nature, we might be walking in safer paths than those into which the social instinct of fear has led us. Possibly, if we thought less, or made less pretence to think, of the material prosperity of our neighbour and more of the health of our own souls, we might ourselves be a little less liable to the temptations of material success at any price. Our scientific efficiency might be directed for the real welfare of society, and we might be in better place to demand the orderly conduct and allegiance of others.

All this is not meant as a plea for inefficiency or for idle revery; nor is it a call to shirk the pressing problems of organization and labour. There is a truth of human nature as there is a science of material forces, and the better efficiency is that of a soul which has first come to terms with itself. Even he who, to those absorbed in business, seems to have withdrawn into the contemplation of ideas as into a harbour of refuge, may have found a certain value in life itself which it were good for the world to understand. But at least, whether for the scholar or for the man of affairs, it looks as if, first of all, we needed somehow or other to get the fear of God back into society.

OXFORD, WOMEN, AND GOD

OXFORD, WOMEN, AND GOD

MRS. HUMPHRY WARD has the unenviable portion of a reformer who wrought manfully — should we say womanfully? — to lead England out of the Cimmerian bogs of Victorianism, yet somehow is heartily despised by the younger generation which walks the sunlit ways of our peaceful, spacious Georgian world. It would be an instructive pastime, with her autobiography in hand, to study the causes of this cruel injustice; but that is another story. My present interest in her autobiography [1] has been centred not so much on her own career as on her account of life in Oxford during the sixties and seventies. The four chapters in which she collects her reminiscences of these years are quite the most entertaining of the record — are, in fact, the only part that offers much entertainment of any sort; and if this were my theme, I might suggest that it was the spell of Oxford, however reformed an Oxford, still haunting her mind that makes her so unacceptable to the very much otherwise reformed young wits now gasping their discontent in London. Her first novel, *Miss Bretherton*, was a tale

[1] *A Writer's Recollections.* By Mrs. Humphry Ward. New York: Harper & Brothers. 1918. — This essay, it need scarcely be noted, was written while Mrs. Ward was living.

of the university, and *Lady Connie*, her latest
novel written before her autobiography, returns
to the same scenes; and these, with the chapters
of her *Recollections*, might give the lie to Andrew
Lang's pleasant witticism that there are no good
books about Oxford because they are all composed by women who have spent one day in —
Cambridge.

Jowett and Mark Pattison are her heroes, the
Master of Balliol in his triumphant days of educational supremacy, and the Rector of Lincoln
socially tamed by the restless, keen, very æstheti-
cal "Mrs. Pat.," yet otherwise savage enough
with his gibes at the unteutonized scholarship of
Balliol and the persistent priestcraft of Christ
Church. But other figures, denizens and visitors,
flit through her pages — Swinburne, Renan,
George Eliot, Mandell Creighton, Taine, Green
— each the subject of an anecdote or the occasion for moralizing. Perhaps the most memorable of these stories is that which reports a conversation with Walter Pater in the days when
the critic had yielded something of his earlier
paganism and was lapsing into a kind of artistic
dalliance with the charms of Christianity. Mrs.
Ward had been proclaiming the near downfall
of orthodoxy and the impossibility of its main-
taining itself long against the attacks from the
historical and literary camps. To her surprise,
Pater shook his head and looked rather troubled.

"'I don't think so,' he said. Then with hesitation: 'And we don't altogether agree. You think it's all plain. But I can't. There are such mysterious things. Take that saying, "Come unto me, all ye that are weary and heavy-laden." How can you explain that? There is a mystery in it — a something supernatural.'"

It was the spirit of the place that would not be exorcised from Pater's thought, and it is curious to observe how this same shadow from the past lay over Mrs. Ward's mind, despite her absorption in modern tendencies and her expressed surprise. She was thinking more of her own young life than of her heroine's when she wrote, in *Lady Connie*, that "in those days Oxford was still praising 'famous men and the fathers who begat' her; their shades still walked her streets." Only Mrs. Ward was rebellious under the spell, while Pater was gently acquiescent. Again she is speaking for herself through the mouth of her heroine: "We who are alive must always fight the past, though we owe it all we have. Oxford has been to me often a witch — a dangerous — almost an evil witch. I seemed to see her — benumbing the young forces of the present. And the scientific and practical men, who would like to scrap her, have sometimes seemed to me right." It is, in fact, just this mingling of the past and the present in her mood that piques our interest; and involuntarily, as we see her picture

of Oxford under Jowett and Pattison, another
picture arises of the city as it was a generation
earlier under Newman and Pusey, and her anec-
dotes of contemporaries recall a host of stories of
the men who preceded or were lingering on as
ghosts of themselves. It is all so much the same,
yet so different. What change has come over the
place so reluctant to change?

If it were my vein to attempt the smart style
now in fashion, I should think it enough to describe the change as consisting in the banishment
of God and the admission of woman. At any
rate, whatever else was happening in Mrs. Ward's
time, the gods were going and women were coming; and of one, at least, of these events she is
fully aware, and might even boast that she was
pars magna. In her maiden days, she says, Oxford was a city of young men, "it was not also a
city of young women, as it is to-day." But they
were already creeping in, and before she left had
conquered the right of domicile, much after the
manner of the fabled camel; in fact the encroachment of the feminine into a society so archaically
masculine is the real theme of her university
novels, and her *Recollections* show how much her
own activities as writer and talker helped on the
invasion. But it was not only the presence of the
undergraduate in petticoats that marked the
revolution; wives, too, were multiplying, and
with them came a great alteration in the habits

of the faculty. In the generation preceding none
of the tutors were married and very few of the
professors; Oxford was still under the old con-
ventual rule, though, with the disappearance of
the religious ideal and purpose of celibacy, the
peculiarly monkish traits of character had vanished and left behind only the bare "character,"
as that word used to be understood. This indeed
is the chief impression one gets from the memoirs
of the age. There was purpose enough in the
lives of Newman and his group, but all about
them was a society of happy egotists whom isolation from the shaping contacts with the world
had allowed to develop each as whim or passion
guided him. Even the throngs of boys, who were
so conspicuous to Mrs. Ward at her first coming,
seem somehow to have been pushed into the
background of the picture by these crusty bachelors. Of a certain "Mo." Griffith, Senior Fellow
of Merton, who used to fly from Oxford in term-
time to avoid the Philistines, as he called the
undergraduates, the story is told that once in
vacation, when dining alone in Hall, he was confronted with the sight of a single scholar who had
not gone down. "Fetch a screen, Manciple!" he
cried. It is the Fellows' side of the screen we see
in the annals of that age.

And one can imagine what went on there on
this occasion, if our Don was faithful to his creed.
It is related that a physician, having dined with

him and eaten too sparingly, excused his absti-
nence by pleading the maxim, "Eat and leave off
hungry." Mo. threw up his hands: "Eat and
leave off hungry! Why not wash and leave off
dirty?" No doubt, too, he would have been
ready, with most of his contemporaries, to exclaim in the same manner over the command to
drink and leave off thirsty — sober their forefathers would have said. For, if the *Logic* of
Dean Aldrich of Christ Church was still after a
century and a half the textbook of Oxford, it is to
be feared that some of the logicians of the day
had not forgotten the Dean's practical example
of the art of ratiocination:

> Si bene quid memini, sunt causæ quinque bibendi:
> Hospitis adventus, præsens sitis atque futura,
> Aut vini bonitas, aut quælibet altera causa —

which may be translated for a less genial and less
erudite generation:

> If I remember well, these be the sum
> Fivefold of drink's occasions and its laws:
> A guest arrived, thirst present or to come,
> Virtue of wine, or any other cause.[1]

The same Moses (or Edward as he chose to call
himself) Griffith was one day walking round

---

[1] The old, freer translation is well known:

> If on my theme I rightly think,
> There are five reasons why men drink:
> Good wine, a friend, because I'm dry,
> Or lest I should be by and by,
> Or any other reason why.

Christ Church Meadow with a brother Fellow named Frowd, who began, as *laudator temporis acti*, to lament the disappearance from Oxford of the strange originals of their younger days. "Does it not occur to you, Dr. Frowd," was the reply, "that you and I are the 'characters' of to-day?" I ask my reader: Does our world, of which we sometimes boast, possess such naïve sublimity of assurance? But Mo. and his friend flattered themselves, if they thought their originality outlawed and peculiar at that date. As I stand in the corner of my library in which the Oxford memoirs of the day are gathered, and as I turn over the pages of book after book looking for examples, I am embarrassed by the need of selection among so many doughty heroes and so many combats of wit. Like Æneas, I see

Battles through all the world made known to fame.

The easiest way out of the difficulty, were it permissible, would be to copy off a chapter of the Reverend W. Tuckwell's *Reminiscences*, and perhaps the best of permissible ways is to direct any reader not already acquainted therewith to that storehouse of entertainment. If there is any more exhilarating book of the sort in English, I do not know it; and if there is a more captivating group of oddities than the scholars who congregated by the Isis before the advent of Mrs. Ward's petticoats, and who live again in Mr.

Tuckwell's memory, I have not met them in my literary pilgrimage. Whatever Oxford may not have been, it was vastly amusing. If our friend Mo. left the impression of a rather gluttonous and bibulous curmudgeon, it is not to be inferred that the story of that society is a mere "gastrology," like the work of the ancient Epicurean who, as Athenæus says, "made a voyage round the inhabited earth for his belly's sake" (I omit the rest of the quotation), and wrote up his adventures in epic form. No, these Dons were true *deipnosophists*, dinner-philosophers, whose talk was as much wittier than their successors' as their appetites were more capacious. Mr. Tuckwell draws the comparison neatly:

The Common Rooms to-day, as I am informed, are swamped by shop; while general society, infinitely extended by the abolition of College celibacy, is correspondingly diluted. Tutors and Professors are choked with distinctions and redundant with educational activity; they lecture, they write, they edit, they investigate, they athleticise, they are scientific or theological or historical or linguistic; they fulfil presumably some wise end or ends. But one accomplishment of their forefathers has perished from among them — they no longer *talk:* the Ciceronian ideal of conversation, σπουδαῖον οὐδέν, φιλόλογα *multa*, "Not a word on shop, much on literature, "has perished from among them. In the Thirties, conversation was a fine art, a claim to social distinction: choice sprouts of the brain, epigram, anecdote, metaphor, now nursed carefully for the printer, were joyously lavished on one another by the men and women of those bibulous, pleasant days, who equipped themselves at leisure for the wit combats each late supper-party provoked.

That is well put, and is in the main true; but I should like to discourse on one of Mr. Tuckwell's points — his unreserved condemnation of "shop," which he connects with rather an unfair translation of Cicero's Greek. The comparative dulness of conversation in the modern Hall, or in the American equivalent, is not to be laid to the intrusion of shop, but to the wrong kind of shop. The minute specializing of studies has brought about such a division of interests among scholars that you will scarcely find any body of men, nominally united, who have less in common intellectually than the faculty of a university. Only the other day I heard a biologist girding at a teacher of Greek for his concern with a remote and outworn civilization. It was easy for the Grecian to retort that after all the polity of the coral insect represented a stage of evolution immensely more antique than the constitution of Athens two thousand years ago, and that the art of Sophocles and the philosophy of Aristotle were closer to the business and bosoms of mankind than the skeleton deposits of the Anthozoan polyp. (Which last heavy-loaded phrase, however, I got from the encyclopædia, not from the professor's lips.) The retort was effective, but it did not bring the two gentlemen closer together.

And so, in the absence of any intellectual meeting-ground, except that of mere transient curiosity, college men are driven to the interchange of personalities and the discussion of departmental wire-pulling, from which their only escape is the political news of the morning paper. Their shop is no better, for conversational purposes, than a department store. But it was not so when scholars were interested in the same group of subjects, with, of course, a human variety of views. Even the personal gossip of such a society took colour from their more serious pursuits; even malice and backbiting spoke the dialect of the Muses, as any one may discover for himself if he will read the memoirs of the day. Mr. Tuckwell, for instance, has a good deal to say of a certain "Horse" Kett, of Trinity, as he was called by reason of a long face dominated by a straight bony nose — an estimable gentleman withal, and not without critical acumen of a sort that won the respect of De Quincey. But his academic renown was owing to that equine countenance and to its power of "inspiring from the seniors jokes in every learned language, and practical impertinences from the less erudite youngsters." This Kett put out a rival to Aldrich's book, which he entitled *Logic Made Easy*. It was a feeble and blundering thing, but provocative of high mirth, when Copleston of Oriel reviewed it in a scathing pamphlet, with the motto —

Aliquis latet error; Equo ne credite, Teucri!

Mr. Tuckwell would have come closer to the
mark if, instead of contrasting shop and literature, he had said that the two were then one
thing. We sometimes speak slightingly of the
erudition of those cloistered Dons, and use their
idleness to point a moral or adorn ourselves; yet
as a matter of fact many of them were prodi-
giously learned — only with a difference. What
they knew, they knew. Perhaps the long-forgot-
ten name of James Endell Tyler may be recalled
as a type. "He was not a reformer of Churches
and creeds," we read of him in Mozley's *Reminiscences*, "but he was an able and effective lec-
turer. He was no genius, it used to be said of
him, but he could construe Thucydides 'through
a deal board.'" No doubt their reading was cir-
cumscribed, but that very circumscription had
its advantages, in so far as it made learning a
bond of sympathy rather than a dyke of separation.[1] The great masters of human experience

[1] One may find an amusing illustration in Mark Pattison's *Memoirs* of the common confusion of mind on this
matter of scholarship. On page 237 he says: "Probably
there was no period of our history during which, I do not
say science and learning, but the ordinary study of the
classics was so profitless or at so low an ebb as during the
period of the Tractarian controversy. By the secession of
1845 this was extinguished in a moment, and from that
moment dates the regeneration of the University." This is
the voice of the anti-theologian. Hear now the words of the

were in their blood; they knew them by heart; thought as they thought; spoke their language, with perfect assurance that the most recondite play of wit or wisdom would be caught up immediately and answered in kind. Some of them may have quoted with the awful profusion of a Porson, who, as Byron declared, "used to recite, or rather vomit, pages of all languages, and could hiccup Greek like a Helot"; but Porson was a Cantabrigian, and a beast; and all good things may be abused — even temperance. And to the drunkenness of Porson we owe, it must be granted, the profoundest utterance of pessimism that has ever fallen from mortal lips. He was in his customary state one night. Wishing to blow out his candle, and seeing, as is said to be the way of the inebriated, two flames side by side where there was only one, he three times directed his swaying steps to the wrong image, and three times blew, with no effect, for the non-existent cannot be extinguished. Whereupon he drew

educator on what is really one aspect of the extinction of the hated movement (p. 240): "The sudden withdrawal of all reverence for the past has generated a type of intellect which is not only offensive to taste but is unsound as training. The young Oxford, which our present system tends to turn out, is a mental form which cannot be regarded with complacency by any one who judges an education, not by its programme, but by its *élèves*. Our young men are not trained; they are only filled with propositions, of which they have never learned the inductive basis." — Might not this second passage have come straight from Newman's *Idea of a University?*

back, balanced himself, and gave verdict:
"Damn the nature of things!" [1]

It may be objected that all this erudition was
sterile; it produced few books, and some of these
were bad. The charge is fair, but there are allevi-
ations. The barrenness is attributable in part to
the kind of scholarship in vogue; it was not the
business of these men to decipher manuscripts
and investigate sources, and when they did turn
to such work they were capable of making a mess
of it. But if they had been better editors, does it
follow necessarily that they would have been
more interesting men? And there was another
cause, a tradition that still lingers at Oxford
through all the changes of the past fifty years.
I remember not long ago talking with an Oxo-
nian, of all places in a New York elevated train,
about these matters. Somehow we had got to the
question of the best model for the writing of
Greek prose, and he appealed to the opinion of
one of his teachers in favour of the simpler narrative style of Thucydides. I had never heard the
scholar's name — nor do I now recall it — and
inquired about him. "Why," said my friend,
"he is probably the most learned man in Oxford,

[1] So the story was once told me on a memorable occasion
by a friend, now one of the editors of the *Weekly Review*,
and so I repeat it. But my genial authority is only a mathe-
matician after all; for another and I fear truer version the
reader must be referred to the Porsoniana at the end of the
Table-Talk of Samuel Rogers.

so nearly omniscient that his colleagues live in constant terror of his criticism." I still expressed my surprise that a pundit of such renown should be unknown to me. "That is not strange," was the reply, "for he has never published anything." My surprise was increased, and I asked the reasons. "Well, you know," said my friend, who to his other charms adds a slight impediment of speech, "it is n't quite g-good form in Oxford to p-print." — A foolish tradition, I dare say; yet I challenge any one familiar with the growing custom among us to appraise a man's academic standing by the quantity of his output — often enough in the form of petty source-hunting — I challenge him to deny that such a tradition has its good side.

It is not to be supposed that the scholarship of Oxford passed without comment at the time. Critics were ready then as now, though with less immediate effect, to denounce the narrow exclusive spirit of the place; and one series of criticisms in particular, appearing in the *Edinburgh Review*, drew out apologies from Copleston, published in 1810 and 11, which contain paragraphs still readable to-day with profit and interest. To the reviewer's charge that classical studies are frivolous because they do not tend directly to what is called practical good, Copleston replies finely with a plea for "cultivation of mind which is itself a good, a good of the highest order, with-

out any immediate reference to bodily appetites
or wants of any kind," and then appeals to what
the Oxford tradition had done for the formation
of character, and specially for character under
the testing strain of war. "If classical education
be regarded in this light," he says, "there is none
in which it will be found more faultless. A high
sense of honour, a disdain of death in a good
cause, a passionate devotion to the welfare of
one's country, a love of enterprise, and a love of
glory, are among the first sentiments which those
studies communicate to the mind. And as their
efficacy is undoubted in correcting the narrow
habits and prejudices to which the separation of
the professions gives birth, so in the rough school
of war is it more especially exemplified in mitigat-
ing the tone of that severe instructor and in soft-
ening some of his harshest features." — Can any
one read the letters of Arthur Heath and of other
Oxonians who went out the other day into the
battle line and did not return, without feeling
that even the remnant of the old tradition has
not lost the power claimed for it by the Provost
of Oriel?

> God rest you, happy gentlemen,
>   Who laid your good lives down,
> Who took the khaki and the gun
>   Instead of cap and gown.
> God bring you to a fairer place
>   Than even Oxford town.

I wish there were space to quote the striking words of Copleston on the mischief, even then threatening, of the undue predominance of Political Economy in education and among "the clamorous sciolists of the day"; what was once prophecy is now fact; but this is not my present theme. It is more to the point to show how the old tradition, with all its exclusions, perhaps on account of them, caught the abler youths of the day — and they are the only ones who count — in its spell and stimulated their ambition. Pusey's mother, who as an old woman loved to talk of her famous son, used to tell how he had asked his father for a complete set of the Fathers as his reward for gaining a First Class; "and how in the Long Vacation he used to carry his folios to a shady corner in the garden which she pointed out, and sit there reading with a tub of cold water close at hand, into which he plunged his curly head whenever study made it ache." Quite as significant is the account of the excitement roused by the success of Jowett, Pusey's lifelong rival, when he won a Balliol Fellowship in 1839. In the candidate's home there is an outburst of joy as great as if he had been appointed Lord Chancellor, and in the university, as one of his friends writes, "nothing has been talked about here so much for a long time. . . . 'Little Jowett' was nearly pulled to pieces." Frankly, do we think so highly of getting a fellowship to-day?

Is the business of education quite so serious an
affair or so enthralling?

Part of that ancient enthusiasm may be explained by the fact that success in the schools was
an open door to the great prizes of State and
Church; it was still true that knowledge of Greek
seemed a proper claim to a bishopric. (I heard
one of our bishops the other day derive "disciple" from the Greek *didasko*, "to teach"!) And
this truth a Winchester lad of the day expressed
with delightful naïveté in the closing lines of an
Address to Learning:

> Make me, O Sphere-descended Queen,
> A Bishop, or at least a Dean.

What prize, if any, his school bestowed on the
poet I do not know, but he ended his well-
planned career as Warden of New College and
Bishop of Chichester. Nor was it the young
visionary alone who beheld Learning as the patron of success. In one of his Christmas sermons
the redoubtable Gaisford (to whom as an undergraduate his Dean had observed, "You will
never be a gentleman, but you may succeed with
certainty as a scholar" — and become yourself a
Dean, he might have added) stated the same
truth with prosaic candour: "Nor can I do better, in conclusion, than impress upon you the
study of Greek literature, which not only ele-
vates above the vulgar herd, but leads not in-

frequently to positions of considerable emolument."

It sounds a little queer and mercenary, put that way, though we can wish that the emoluments of scholarship were rather more considerable to-day; but there is another version of Gaisford's words — I do not know which of the two is *verbatim* correct — which sets the matter in a different light. According to this report his exhortation to the study of Greek was on the ground that it would enable a man "not only to read the oracles of God in the original, but also to look down with contempt upon the vulgar herd." And on the whole this second version is the fairer representation of the spirit of the age. Lawn sleeves may have been a pleasant, and quite legitimate, incentive to the young student poring on his Aristotle and Origen, but I think he went to those great philosophers and theologians seeking first the oracles of God. I have said much of the more eccentric, even the coarser, habits of these cloistered scholars. We must take the good with the bad, and I fear that the old charge made in the time of Charles II might still be repeated of a certain Oxford set: "At a dingy, horrid, scandalous ale-house over against the college, Balliol men by perpetual 'bubbeing' added art to their natural stupidity to make themselves perfect sots." Yet there was another side even to the indulgence in Port.

"Narratur et prisci Catonis
Sæpe mero caluisse virtus, —

with all its faults there is something generous
about it, and if the Latin proverb says right, it is
at least no enemy to truth," was the reply of
Copleston to the *Edinburgh* reviewer who had
scourged the university for its guzzling. Though
a sprinkling of "bubbeing" sots was to be reckoned with, nevertheless the real mark of this society was its conviction that it held a place set
apart amid a world of indifference, as guardian
of the truth; it still believed that scholarship was
primarily concerned with the oracles of God. If
we look below the surface, we shall find the very
zest of those quaint characters that move through
the memoirs of the day in their extraordinary
mingling of personal eccentricity with religious
regularity. Nor must we forget that the Oxford
of Mo. Griffith and his brother oddity was also
the home of Newman and Keble and Pusey, in
whom, however we may be disposed towards
their particular dogmas, we must acknowledge
that the zeal of God burned with a steady, almost a devouring, flame.

But perhaps the best type of the Oxford I have
in mind is not one of those eagles of the faith, but
their servant and drudge in the intellectual battle, if I may so designate Charles Marriott without injustice to his noble simplicity. Eccentric he
was, almost beyond credence. In the street his

strange figure could be recognized afar by its involved mufflings of cloak and wrapper and veil.
Indoors he wore a black silk skull-cap, which,
from his habit of slumbering in public places,
might often be seen nodding, with the drollest
effect — yet somehow he contrived to hear more
in his sleep, and remember better, than other
men who listened with head erect. His somno-
lence, apparently, was only a deeper lapse in his
normal state of absent-mindedness. If accosted
suddenly in the street he would start and stare at
you for a moment in utter silence, as though he
had been walking awake in some other world, as
no doubt he had been. And like the man were his
rooms. In a biographical sketch, aptly entitled
The Man of Saintly Life, Dean Burgon gives a
vivid account of one of Marriott's breakfasts, to
which, as usual, the careless host had invited
guest after guest at random with no thought of
their number. What happened may be told in
Burgon's own words:

On entering the dear man's rooms next morning,
whereas breakfast had been laid for ten, [we found] fifteen guests had already assembled. While we were secretly counting the teacups, another rap was heard, and
in came two University Professors. All laughed: but it
was no laughing matter, for still another and another
person presented himself. The bell was again and again
rung: more and more tea and coffee, — muffins and dry
toast, — butter and bread, — cream and eggs, — chops
and steaks, — were ordered; and "Richard" was begged
to "spread my other table-cloth on my other table."

The consequence was that our Host's violoncello, —
fiddle-strings and music-books, — printers' proofs and
postage stamps, — medicine-bottles and pill-boxes, —
respirator and veil, — gray wrapper for his throat and
green shade for his eyes, — pamphlets and letters innumerable, — *all* were discharged in a volley on to the
huge sofa. At last, by half-past nine (thanks to Richard's superhuman exertions) twenty of us (more or less)
sat down to breakfast.... I am bound to say that the
meal was an entire success, — as far as the strangers
were concerned. They were greatly entertained, — in
more senses than one.

Yet this same absentee from the world was a
scholar of indefatigable industry, to whom Newman and Pusey could always turn for any oner-
ous task of editing or translating in their paper
warfare with rationalism. Nor would it be easy
to say where, with such a man, scholarship ended
and saintship began, so thoroughly were heart
and brain in accord. He was one in whom the
thought of self was lost in uninterrupted contemplation of God, one in whom the consumma-
tion of Aristotle's *theoria* might seem to have
been realized in Christian worship. "There was,"
says one who knew him well, "something un-
speakably sweet and pure and simple, in the outcome of his habitual inner life.... To me he
seemed habitually to walk with God.... He was
of a kindred nature to the Saint who said, 'When
I am in heaviness I will think upon God'; and
who habitually spoke of God as 'his stronghold

whereunto he might always resort, his house of defence and his castle.'"

Now what strikes one in the Oxford of Mrs. Ward, as it would strike one still more in the Oxford of to-day, is the impossibility of meeting with such a character as that of Marriott: the eccentricity is gone, vanished with the last relics of medieval isolation; gone, too, the spiritual sense of an actual presence of the Deity. As for the eccentricity, its disappearance, Mrs. Ward herself would probably admit, was caused in no small measure by the influx of women into a society of bachelors. With petticoats came the world and the conventions of the world; manners were softened, the tongue was filed, angles of originality were ironed out; the drawing-room conquered the cloister. As for the second change, whether the intrusion of women had anything to do with the synchronous extrusion of God, you will not hear from me; even if I believed in such a causal relation, I have too many misoneistic quarrels already in hand to risk the charge of misogyny. But I can tell you what Mrs. Ward would say: she would simply deny the fact of extrusion. That the religiosity of Newman and Pusey had been expelled, she would grant, and would boast, with reason, that her own pen had been one of the effective instruments of the expulsion; but she would uphold her sincere conviction that the idea of God had been merely puri-

fied by the process. For such a tenet she does
actually argue vehemently in a dialogue on *The
New Reformation* contributed to the *Nineteenth
Century* for March, 1889, as part of the acrid debate then waging between Huxley and the enemies of agnosticism. "The point is," she declares, in reply to the fears of orthodoxy — "the
point is, What religion is possible to men, for
whom God is the only reality, and Jesus that
friend of God and man, in whom, through all
human and necessary imperfection, they see the
natural leader of their inmost life?" And, more
succinctly, she adds: "God — though I can find
no names for Him — is more real, more present
to me than ever before." In like manner, with
tacit reference to the criticisms that still ema-
nated from the unreformed stronghold of Christ
Church, she dwells in her *Recollections* on the
deep religious spirit of her beloved heretic,
Jowett:

If ever a man was *Gottbetrunken*, it was the Master,
many of whose meditations and passing thoughts, withdrawn, while he lived, from all human ken, yet written
down — in thirty or forty volumes! — for his own discipline and remembrance, can now be read, thanks to his
biographers, in the pages of his *Life*. They are extraor-
dinarily frank and simple; startling, often, in their bare-
ness and truth. But they are, above all, the thoughts of
a mystic, moving in a Divine presence. An old and intimate friend of the Master's once said to me that he
believed "Jowett's inner mind, especially towards the

end of his life, was always in an attitude of Prayer. One would go and talk to him on University or College business in his study, and suddenly see his lips moving, slightly and silently, and know what it meant."

Now that there is an element of truth in what Mrs. Ward maintains, I would not deny; yet as I read the life of Jowett I cannot divest myself of the feeling that his religion is a kind of reverberation from forces which have ceased to operate — like the prolonged intonation of a bell after the last stroke of the hammer. It was Jowett who avowed that "Voltaire has done more good than all the Fathers of the Church put together"; and as he grew older his faith took on more and more the form of a belief with nothing to believe. "Litanies should have no creeds"; all dogmas, including belief in a personal God and in immortality, should be surrendered, and in their place religion should be steadied on what he understood — erroneously, it must be added — as Buddhistic nihilism. The "Divine presence" with him was "mystic"; what, one asks, was actually present? No doubt Jowett continued in the habit of inner worship, but the shrine before which his lips moved in meditation was empty, and what vitality his faith possessed was drawn, vampire-like, from the heart of the men whose creed he had shattered. No doubt the idea of Deity, as Mark Pattison declared, misapplying a phrase of Coleridge's, had been "defæcated to a

pure transparency"; would it be unfair to reply
that a pure transparency, so far as our corporeal
or spiritual vision is concerned, means only a
vacuum? The Oxford of Newman may have
been superstitious; the Oxford of Jowett, despite
Mrs. Ward's protests, was rapidly becoming
Godless. The new scholarship is busied with investigation of sources and scientific phenomena,
and has no need of the hypothesis of a divine
presence. So far as religion prevails, it is the religion of humanity, such as that for which Mrs.
Ward pleaded in *Robert Elsmere*, not Newman's
religion of God and the individual human soul.
Worship has been transferred from the pulpit of
Saint Mary's to the recreation room of the Pass-
more Edwards Settlement.

What this change means to education I have
found curiously intimated in one of the smart
sayings of Stephen McKenna's *Sonia*. He has
been describing his experience in an East End
university mission, where, as he says, thirty per
cent of his Oxford generation worked for longer
or shorter periods, and he concludes: "I doubted,
and still doubt, the possibility of friendship between a Shadwell stevedore and the angular, repellent product of an English public school and
university; this is not to put one above the other,
but merely to disbelieve the existence of a common intellectual currency." — *Not to put one
above the other:* can you imagine a scholar of

Gaisford's generation doubting in his mind whether the product of Winchester and Oxford, *ceteris paribus*, is higher than the product of the Shadwell docks? Yet just such a query, in less paradoxical terms, you may find in almost every recent book that reveals what is going on inside the minds of serious university men. Even Jowett could exclaim over his college as "a bad school for character," where a "sort of weak cleverness" is fostered and "manliness" is impaired. If the modern report of university life is true, I wonder why we go on spending millions of dollars and pounds to maintain institutions which make men no better than stevedores, and why, on the other hand, we waste so much sympathy on life at the docks which makes men no worse than professors. Our ears have grown too squeamish to endure Gaisford's blunt association of the oracles of God with contempt for the vulgar herd, nor do I think his a happy or a true definition of the aims of education; but one thing is certain: if the college as an institution is to retain any value above the shop and the marketplace, if the pursuit of scholarship as an end in itself is to offer any satisfaction for the finer spirits of men, then, in some way, those studies must be restored to authority which give zest and significance to the inner life of the soul; and at the centre of that life, binding all its interests into one, lifting them above the grosser forms of utility, irradiating them with joy, must be the idea of God.

I did not intend, when I began this account of Oxford before and after the reforms of the mid-nineteenth century, to end on so solemn an argument. What impressed me most while going through Mrs. Ward's *Recollections* and recalling the reminiscences of the preceding generation, was the simple fact that college society as portrayed in these books had grown in a few years comparatively less amusing to read about and distinctly less interesting to itself. I do not mean that Mrs. Ward's chapters are without entertainment — I have said they were the most entertaining part of her memoir — but the college life she depicts has lost much of its peculiar tang and proud independence; already its main significance is in the comparison it evokes. The change, I think, will scarcely be disputed by any one conversant with the literature, though some may contend that the loss of interest is more than compensated by the suppression of quaint or ludicrous eccentricities. For my part I would not hold a brief for mere eccentricity, however fond I may be of the well-crusted "character." But that is only half the story. The waning of interest, in its deeper aspect, is typical of an intellectual revolution which has grown more and more evident with the passing of the years, until now the ancient pride of the scholar and the self-content of the scholar's career seem to have been swallowed up in the one prevailing note of distaste and dissatisfaction and apology. Professor Gilbert Murray, who is qualified to speak for the Oxford of to-day, complains of the satiety that pervades college life, and attributes it to the very liberation of mind and the enriching of the means of personal satisfaction. "Whatever gifts Oxford may bring her children," he says, "she is apt to bring steeped in the one poison that is fatal to poetry, the poison of satiety. A spirit of satiety broods over the rich meadows and the slow streams, over streets and towers and quadrangles and playing-grounds. Do you wish for games? There they are waiting for you, laid on like water or electric light, all the games that exist. If you can think of another it shall be brought; there shall be no trouble to you in the preparing of it, and no time for your hunger to grow. Do you wish for books? There they are, old and new, in convenient libraries and magnificent bookshops, more than you can ever read or look at; so many that the sight wearies you, and suggests, not a desire to be richly gratified, but an ever-mounting and fastidious duty." This is no doubt a true account of the matter, true in a way; but going back to an earlier day, and studying the transition from the Oxford of Newman to the Oxford of Mrs. Ward, I seem to see other causes at work than that heaping up of material resources which has turned the delight of scholarship into a fastidious duty. At least one can safely say that a unique interest was lost to learning with the admission of women into Oxford's cloistered society and the banishment of God.

THE END

INDEX TO SHELBURNE ESSAYS

Index to Shelburne Essays

ELEVEN VOLUMES

The Riverside Press
CAMBRIDGE . MASSACHUSETTS
U . S . A